## MAZELTOV!

More ethnic hilarity from the world's best-selling humorist!

*  *  *

A Jewish woman in the Bronx recently caused quite a commotion by revealing the contents of her will. First, she stipulated that she be cremated. Then, she asked that her ashes be spread over Bloomingdale's so she'd be assured of having her daughter visit her at least twice a week.

*  *  *

**Books by Larry Wilde**

*The Official Polish/Italian Joke Book*
*The Official Jewish/Irish Joke Book*
*The Official Virgins/Sex Maniacs Joke Book*
*The Official Black Folks/White Folks Joke Book*
*MORE The Official Polish/Italian Joke Book*
*The Official Democrat/Republican Joke Book*
*The Official Religious/NOT SO Religious Joke Book*
*The Official Smart Kids/Dumb Parents Joke Book*
*The Official Golfers Joke Book*
*The LAST Official Polish Joke Book*
*The Official Dirty Joke Book*
*The Official Cat Lovers/Dog Lovers Joke Book*
*The LAST Official Italian Joke Book*

and

The 1979 Official Ethnic Calendar

also

*The Complete Book of Ethnic Humor* (Corwin Books)
*How the Great Comedy Writers Create Laughter*
  (Nelson-Hall)
*The Great Comedians* (Citadel Press)

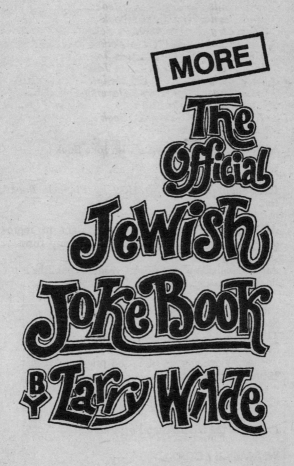

MORE
The Official Jewish Joke Book

by Larry Wilde

PINNACLE BOOKS • LOS ANGELES

For beautiful Aunt Bella—
a gray-haired Jewish lady
with sparkling Irish eyes
and a heart full of love for
all humanity.

# About the Author

Comedian Larry Wilde has been making people laugh for over twenty-five years in America's top nightclubs and hotels as well as on comedy records and television commercials and sit-coms. *MORE The Official Jewish/Irish Joke Book* represents the fourteenth humor collection by the prolific Californian. With book sales of over 3,500,000 Larry Wilde has become the best-selling humorist in the world.

Mr. Wilde has further distinguished himself in the field of humor as the author of two definitive works on comedy: *The Great Comedians* (Citadel) and *How the Great Comedy Writers Create Laughter* (Nelson-Hall).

His latest contribution to the comedic art form is a hardbound collection of jokes representing over twenty minority groups: *The Complete Book of Ethnic Humor* (Corwin Books).

Born in Jersey City, New Jersey, Larry spent two years in the United States Marine Corps and then received his liberal arts degree from the University of Miami, Florida.

The author resides in Los Angeles with his wife, the former Maryruth Poulos of Hanna, Wyoming. Mrs. Wilde is a gourmet cook and is currently preparing a humorous ethnic cookbook.

# INTRODUCTION

When the first *Official Jewish/Irish Joke Book* was published in 1974, neither the publisher nor the author had any way of anticipating the reaction by readers. (It is now in its sixth printing with sales of over 500,000.)

Market research is underway to determine how many people bought the book for the Jewish half or the Irish half and how many bought the whole enchilada. However, several facts have already come to light:

1) Unlike the reaction by some Polish groups (to the three *Official Polish Joke Books*) there has not been one single objection voiced by any Jewish or Irish organization.

2) Israel and Ireland continue to be an excellent source for laughter despite the turmoil and unrest in both countries.

3) The well-documented Jewish/Irish sense of humor is probably the most keenly developed of all the minorities.

Though not apparent on the surface, there is a huge similarity between Jewish and Irish humor. Both peoples share an enduring affinity from the painful experiences of privation, prejudice, and religious persecution. Yet they are able to withstand these human tragedies and even jest about it. Actually, they have become enormously skilled at extracting humor from suffering.

In both halves of this book you will find fun

being poked at death, wakes, funerals, religion, rabbis, priests, and sex—all the taboo subjects some people of other nationalities would be afraid to ridicule.

Jewish and Irish humor should be savored like fine wine; for just as the juice of the grapes grows more delicious with age, so do jokes and stories that have at their core the idiosyncrasies of these two great ethnic groups.

There is a classic Irish toast that goes:

> *May you get to heaven a half hour*
> *before the devil knows you're dead.*

An old Yiddish expression from the *Talmud*, freely translated, says:

> *You should live and be well—*
> *And laugh a little too—it couldn't hurt!*

Put the two together and you have the essence of the Jewish/Irish comedic spirit: Be alive! Love! Laugh! Have fun and beat the devil too! Now just begin reading and see. . . .

LARRY WILDE
Los Angeles 1979

MORE
The Official Jewish Joke Book

# Contents

# THE CHILDREN OF ISRAEL

A Christian visiting the Holy Land struck up a conversation with a Palestinian.

"I'm really surprised that you and the Arabs can't get together peacefully."

"My dear man," said the Israeli, "the Jews are a very argumentative people. The only thing you can get two Jews to agree upon is what a third Jew should give to charity."

\*    \*    \*

The voice of the stewardess on the Israeli charter airliner came over the loudspeaker: "Welcome on board. Your hostesses are Mrs. Dora Fein and Mrs. Fay Hershberg and, of course, my son, the pilot."

Two Christians, Walters and Smythe, met on a pilgrimage to Palestine during Holy Week.

"It's a shame all those differences between the Arabs and the Israelis," said Walters.

"Yes," agreed Smythe, "They ought to settle their problems in a true Christian spirit."

\* \* \*

Every year, dignitaries of the Church come from Rome to Israel and a time-honored ceremony is reenacted. One of the chief rabbis hands a jewel-covered scroll to a visiting priest who holds the scroll for a minute, shakes his head, and then returns it to the rabbi until the next year.

This year, however, the rabbi and the priest involved in the ceremony grew curious about the scroll and decided to open it. They removed the jeweled covering, then unrolled yards and yards of yellowed parchment with long columns of numbers on it and some blurred words. The rabbi put on his glasses and finally managed to read the ancient Hebrew letters. It was the bill for the Last Supper.

Kay Rappeport, the jolly Little Rock, Arkansas, KLAZ radio producer, sent along this jovial joke:

Why did the Jews win the Middle East War in 6 days?

Because the equipment was rented!

* * *

New Yorker Friedman joined the Israeli Army. After a week he asked for a 3-day leave of absence.

"What are you, nuts?" the Colonel asked. "You're in the army a week and already you want a pass? To get a 3-day pass you have to do something sensational."

The next day Friedman came back to camp driving an Arab tank. "How did you do it?" asked the amazed Colonel.

"I took one of our tanks and drove toward Jordan," said Friedman. "I saw one of their tanks coming toward me. The Arab put up a white flag, and I put up a white flag. I said to him, 'Do you want to get a 3-day pass?' He said, 'Yes,' so we exchanged tanks."

Miriam Udell, the bouncy Brooklyn homemaker, tells about Fishbeck and Bloomberg who migrated to Israel and became bounty hunters. They were offered $25 for each Arab they captured.

On their first night out they went to sleep on the Left Bank. The next morning Fishbeck woke up and discovered they were surrounded by 10,000 Arabs.

"Wake up," cried Fishbeck, "Wake up! We're rich!"

\* \* \*

*"Wake up, wake up! We're rich!"*

# ISRAELI NAVY SLOGAN

*Don't Give Up the Ship—Sell It*

\* \* \*

Mintz, a former New York dress manufacturer, joined the Israeli Navy on maneuvers in the Mediterranean. Mintz was the lookout on deck of a submarine, the captain down below. Peering through his binoculars, Mintz suddenly froze in fear. He grabbed the speaking tube and shouted, "Captain, on the horizon, a destroyer, it's Egyptian. Fire a torpedo!"

"Okay, Mintz, I'll keep watch on my radar."

A few minutes later. "Captain, two hundred yards away, the enemy. Fire a torpedo!"

"Okay, Mintz, I have him sighted on my radar. I know when to act. Relax."

"Captain, a hundred yards away, a boat, Egyptian. Fire a torpedo!"

"Relax, Mintz, I know when."

"Captain, fifty yards away, an Egyptian boat! Fire a torpedo! I'll pay for it!"

Pushkin and Karpinsky, two refugees, were working on the Negev. They were tired and weary trying to make the desert bloom. "Who needs it?" said Pushkin. "So we were persecuted a little in Russia, but who worked so hard?"

"You jerk," said Karpinsky, "don't you realize that Moses walked 40 years, day and night, just to get here? This is the Promised Land."

"Listen," said Pushkin, "if Moses had walked a few more days we'd be on the Riviera right now."

*　*　*

Eisenstein, aged and bearded, stood in a crowded bus that was making its way through traffic from Jaffa to Tel Aviv.

A 10-year-old boy, unable to reach the straps to balance himself, was hanging on to the man's beard for support.

After awhile the old man couldn't take it any longer. "Say, boy," asked Eisenstein, "would you mind letting go of my beard?"

"What's the matter?" answered the youngster, "are you getting off here?"

Jacobs and Lipkin, two Israeli commandos, were about to be shot by the Arabs.

Jacobs said, "I think I'm gonna ask for a blindfold."

Lipkin said, "Jake, don't make trouble."

\* \* \*

A small vessel was sailing in Israeli water when a Jewish boat pulled alongside. A man on the deck of the sailboat yells, "Ahoy."

A sailor on the Israeli boat shouted back, "Ahoy, yoi, yoi!"

\* \* \*

An Israeli bomber pilot radioed his base commander, "I'm flying over a brand new steel mill built for the Egyptians by the Russians on the Upper Nile and I've got 3 bombs left. Shall I blow up the mill?"

"Don't be a dumbbell!" answered the commander. "Leave that mill alone. Mismanaging it will cost the Arabs at least $10 million a year!"

Kornblum, aged 76, took an unscheduled flight in the Middle East and suddenly found that two big Arabs had also boarded the airplane. One of them said, "Hey, Jew, we want the window seat!" So he gave it to them.

The plane took off and one of the Arabs said, "Go to the back of the plane and get me some coffee!" Kornblum got the coffee and when he came back the other Arab said, "Now *I* want coffee!"

The old man rushed back and got him some, but by the time he got back the fellow's companion wanted a refill. The two kept him running back and forth for an hour. Finally, Kornblum flopped down in a seat, exhausted. One of the Arabs said, "Jew, what do you think of the world?"

"Well, it's in terrible shape," said Kornblum. "In India, Mohammedans are killing Muslims. In Ireland, Protestants are killing Catholics. And in airplanes Jews are pissing in Arabs' coffee!"

*     *     *

How do they take the census in Israel? They roll a nickel down the street.

Berkowitz, a salesman, while driving through the Negev desert, saw an Arab lying on the sand. Berkowitz rushed to the man's side and lifted him up. The Arab whispered, "Water, Effendi, Water!"

"This is Kismet," exclaimed Berkowitz. "Are you in luck. I happen to have in my suitcase the finest selection of ties you ever saw."

"No," wailed the Arab, "Water! Water!"

"These ties you could see right now in the King David Hotel—$15 a piece, for *you* only $10!"

"Please, Effendi, I need water!"

"Look, you seem like a nice person. I'm known all over the Negev as 'Honest Abe.' Whatever kind of ties you like—silk, wool, rep, crepe—you can have what you want . . . $8 each!"

"I need w-w-water!"

*(con't)*

"I need water!"

"All right, you drive a hard bargain. Tell you what—take your pick. Two for $10."

"Pul—eeze, give me water!"

"Oh, you want water?" said Berkowitz. "Why didn't you say so? All you gotta do is crawl 500 feet to that sand dune, hang a right for a quarter of a mile, you'll come to Poopy's Pyramid Club. He'll give you all the water you want!"

The Arab slowly crawled to the sand dune, turned right and with his last remaining strength came to the door of the club. Poopy, the owner, was standing out front. "Water! Water!" begged the Arab.

"You want water? You came to the right place! I got well water, seltzer water, whatever water you want, I got on the inside. The only thing is—you can't go in without a tie."

*"You can't go in . . ."*

The Israelis are very critical of their government leaders. One former prime minister, who has since died, was always being berated for his inability to make a decision.

As a resident of Jerusalem once said, "When he goes to a restaurant and the waiter asks, 'Tea or coffee?' he always answers, 'Half and half!'"

*  *  *

Private Goldman stood guard on one side of a hill.

On the opposite side was an Arab guard.

Goldman kept shouting, "Thirteen! Thirteen! Thirteen!"

The annoyed Arab guard called over, "What are you screaming out 'Thirteen' all the time for? What does that mean?"

"Come over here," said Goldman, "I'll show you."

The Arab guard climbed up and the Israeli said, "Look over that side."

Goldman kicked the Arab over the top and began hollering, "Fourteen! Fourteen! Fourteen!"

16

Fogel, a native of Haifa, passed away and went below. He was amazed to discover lush vegetation, rambling brooks, and pretty little lakes that surrounded him everywhere.

"You look surprised," said an Arab resident of the place.

"I expected Hell to be hot and dry and arid," said the Israeli, "but here are fruit trees, vegetables, flowers, and green grass. You call this Hell?"

"Well, it used to be hot and barren," explained the Arab. "But then those Israelis started coming down here and they irrigated the hell out of the place!"

* * *

Outside a Dublin pub a man put a gun to McQuillan's head and demanded an answer, "Are you a Catholic or a Protestant?"

*Oh, God,* thought the poor Irishman, *if I say Catholic I might get it. If I say Protestant he'll kill me.* He turned to the man who threatened him and said, "Well, O'im an Arab!"

"Oh, my," exclaimed the man, "ain't I the luckiest Israeli in Ireland."

## HEARD ON ISRAELI RADIO:

"This is Station KVY, Tel Aviv, 1400 on your dial, but for you 1395!"

* * *

Morty Bass, the laughing lingerie mogul, entertains buyers with this magnificent bit of merriment:

Old Mrs. Abramson stood at the Wailing Wall hysterically crying and pounding the bricks. A tourist walked over to her and said, "Madam, there's no need for you to cry. The Jews now have a homeland, a place to go to. After 2000 years you finally have the country you've always wanted. Good heavens, why are you crying?"

The old lady said, "I want to go to Miami Beach!"

* * *

At Lockheed a part was needed for a new airplane, and an announcement was sent around the world in order to get the lowest bid. From Poland came a bid of $3000. England offered to build the part for $6000. The asking price from Israel was $9000.

Richardson, the engineer in charge of constructing the new plane, decided to visit each country to find the reason behind the disparity of the bids. In Poland, the manufacturer explained, "$1000 for the materials needed, $1000 for the labor, and $1000 for overhead and a tiny profit."

In England, Richardson inspected the part and found that it was almost as good as the Polish-made one. "Why are you asking $6000?" inquired the engineer.

"$2000 for material," explained the Englishman, "$2000 for labor and $2000 for our expenses and a small profit."

In Israel, the Lockheed representative wandered through a back alley, into a small shop and encountered an elderly man who had submitted the bid of $9000. "Why are you charging that much?" he asked.

"Well," said the old Jew, "$3000 for you, $3000 for me and $3000 for the schlemiel in Poland."

The Israeli Army ordered some surplus tanks from the Italians. Major Rosenberg, the officer making the purchase, noticed there were 2 different models, one $50 less than the other.

"Why two models?" he asked Russo, the Italian in charge.

"For the extra $50," replied Russo, "you get back-up lights."

"Give us the less expensive brand," said the Israeli, "and sell the others to the Egyptians!"

\* \* \*

# BUSINESS IS BUSINESS

Two cloak and suit manufacturers, Ornstein and Raskin, were sitting in their empty offices wailing over the sudden drop in business. "I wish Gabriel would blow his horn," said Ornstein.

"Why?" asked Raskin.

"All the dead people'll come to life," explained Ornstein, "and they'll all need clothes."

\* \* \*

Resnick and Schechter, two garment men, were sitting in a restaurant during the slack season.

"Did you hear about Sidney?" asked Resnick. "His place burned down."

"Yeah?" said Schechter. "He's a nice fellow. He deserves it."

During the French Revolution, when the guillotine was being used almost around the clock, Slutsky lived in a small village outside of Paris. One morning he met Flambeau, who had just returned from the city.

"What's happening there in Paris?" asked Slutsky.

"Conditions are absolutely horrible," replied the Frenchman. "They're cutting off heads by the thousands."

"*Oy*," moaned Slutsky "and me in the hat business!"

\* \* \*

One bright school morning the teacher turned to her class and asked, "All those pupils who want to go to Heaven, raise your hands."

All hands except little Melvin's went up.

The teacher asked him, "Don't you want to go to Heaven?"

"I heard my father tell my mother 'Business has gone to Hell,'" replied Melvin, "and I want to go where the business went."

Nathan and Ira had been partners for years and now Ira lay dying. Nathan stood at his hospital bedside. "I have a confession to make," said Ira, "I robbed our firm of $100,000. I sold the secret formula to our competitors. I took the letter from your desk that your wife needed to get her divorce. And Nathan, I..."

"It's all right," said his partner. "It was me that poisoned you!"

* * *

Business had been terrible for Blum and he cut down on his help. In a month he had to cut down still further, and everyone said that this terrible strain became a fixation that hastened his death a few weeks afterward.

As they were carrying his body down the aisle of the chapel, Blum suddenly sat up in the coffin and asked, "How many men are carrying me?"

"There are eight pallbearers, Mr. Blum," said the undertaker.

"Better lay off two," said Blum lying down again.

Esther Perlmutter, the benevolent Beverly Hills socialite, gets belly laughs with this beaut:

Their ship down, Finkel and Klein were lost on the ocean, clinging to a life raft. Both were pretty tired when suddenly Klein saw a vessel and shouted, "A sail, a sail!"

"So what?" answered Finkel. "We ain't got any samples."

"*. . . and we ain't got any samples!*"

Rosenfeld had a thriving dry goods and clothing business. However, the prosperity was too good to last. A competitor moved in on his left and another on his right. One day the rival on the right erected a huge sign that said:

WE HAVE MADE A TERRIBLE MISTAKE
MUST VACATE
HIGHEST VALUE CLOTHING
AT LOWEST PRICES

A few hours later the competitor on Rosenfeld's left, not to be outdone, also put up a banner:

BANKRUPT SALE—CLOSING OUT
AT LESS THAN COST

Before the business day was over, Rosenfeld handled the opposition by putting this sign over his shop:

MAIN ENTRANCE
TO
THE BIG SALE

*Customer*: Is this suit all wool?

*Edelman*: I won't lie to you. It's not. The buttons are made of silk.

* * *

Cantrowitz and Berkman were discussing their bosses. "My boss," said Cantrowitz, "is such a cheapskate, he should only drop dead!"

"My boss is different," smiled Berkman. "You just can't help liking him. 'Cause if you don't he fires you!"

* * *

"I can't understand why you failed in business."

"Too much advertising."

"You never spent a cent in your life on advertising."

"That's true, but my competitor did."

* * *

*Customer*: If that coat cost you $50 how can you afford to sell it to me for $30?

*Shenberg*: Sh-h-h, my friend. I sell a lot of coats. That's how I can do it!

Shirley Saltzman, the lovely Manhattan homemaker, heard this howler from her accounting whiz hubby, Paul:

*Marvin*: You and I use the same call girl and I happen to know she charges you, a bookkeeper, twice as much as me. Don't you object?

*Barney*: Why should I? I use the double entry system.

\* \* \*

Lerner owned a store that had recently been burglarized. He met Fishman, a friend, on the street.

"I am sorry to hear about the robbery," said Fishman. "Did you lose much?"

"Some," replied the storekeeper. "But it would've been a lot worse if the burglar had broken in the night before."

"Why?" asked the friend.

"Well, you see," said Lerner, "just the day of the robbery I marked everything down 20 percent."

Feinstein, the dress manufacturer, kept a goldfish in a bowl on his desk. One day his sales manager noticed it. "What's that for?"

"It's nice, replied Feinstein, "to have something around that opens their mouth without asking for a raise."

\* \* \*

WINDOW SIGN IN KORNFELD'S
CLOTHING STORE
USE OUR EASY CREDIT PLAN: 100
PERCENT DOWN
NOTHING TO PAY EACH MONTH!

\* \* \*

Plotkin and Singer, two garment manufacturers, met on Seventh Avenue.

"Good morning!" offered Plotkin.

"Don't talk to me," replied Singer. "You're so crooked that the wool you've been pulling over my eyes is 50 percent polyester."

Benny Wildman, the New Jersey men's clothing mogul, manufactured this rollicking mirthful:

Finkelstein was frantic. For five weeks he hadn't been able to do any business because he'd forgotten the combination to the safe.

Rifkin, his partner, had gone to the Catskills for a vacation and there was no word from him. Then one day the phone rang.

"Thank God you called," Finkelstein shouted into the phone. "I can't do any business. I had to lay off the whole shop, fire the salesmen, refuse orders from our biggest accounts, and just stay here in the office and wait for your call."

"What happened?" asked Rifkin.

"It's the safe. I forgot the combination."

"But it's so simple. Turn once left and twice right."

"But what about the numbers?"

"It doesn't matter," answered Rifkin. "The lock's broken."

*"The lock's broken!"*

Mendelbaum had worked a lifetime without ever taking time off.

The doctor suggested he take his first vacation in Palm Beach. Mendelbaum, carrying a large bucket, walked up to the lifeguard.

"How much would it cost for a pail of salt water?" he asked. "I want to take a little sponge bath back at the motel!"

"A dollar a bucket," said the guard, collecting the money from his easy mark.

The next morning, bucket in hand, Mendelbaum showed up again, but now the tide was out about 800 feet. "Hey, lifesaver!" said Mendelbaum. "You certainly are doing a big business!"

* * *

Fliegelman, a big manufacturer of ladies' dresses in New York, received word that his top traveling salesman had died of a heart attack in a Dallas hotel.

Fliegelman, sent this telegram—collect:

RETURN SAMPLES BY FREIGHT AND
SEARCH HIS PANTS FOR ORDERS.

Margolis was selling his bosom buddy a suit. "I'm telling you, Manny," he said, "that even your best friend won't recognize you in that suit! Just take a walk outside for a minute and get the feel of it."

Manny went out and returned a moment later. Margolis rushed up to him.

"Good morning, stranger," he beamed. "What can I do for you?"

\*　　\*　　\*

Rafferty went to Cooperman's Clothing Store to buy a new suit for a wedding.

"You look like a real gentleman," said Cooperman. "Why don't you let me make you a special suit to order?"

"I don't think so," said the Irishman.

"Just tell me what kind of material you like. I'll write to England. They'll get the wool, then they'll weave the cloth, they'll ship it over. I make a pattern, you'll come in for two or three fittings and the suit'll be gorgeous!"

"But I need the suit in three days."

"Don't worry! You'll have it!"

Hornstein manufactured coats but business was so bad the poor man couldn't sleep.

"Count sheep," advised Slodnick, his friend. "It's the best-known cure."

"What can I lose?" signed Hornstein. "I'll try tonight."

The next morning he looked more bleary-eyed than ever. "What happened?" asked Slodnick.

"Sheep I should count," moaned Hornstein. "I counted up to 50,000. Then I sheared the sheep, and made up 50,000 overcoats. Then came the problem that kept me awake all the rest of the night: Where could I get 50,000 linings?"

\* \* \*

A train in Arizona was boarded by robbers, who went through the pockets of the luckless passengers. Greenblatt, a traveling salesman from New York, pulled out $200, but quickly took $4 from the pile and placed it in his vest pocket.

"What'd you do that for?" asked the holdup man, waving his revolver.

"My friend," replied the salesman, "certainly you wouldn't refuse me 2 percent discount on a strictly cash transaction like this?"

*　　*　　*

Dugan, a delivery man from near Hyannisport making his first trip to New York, saw the sign CLIMB ONE FLIGHT AND SAVE $40 ON A NEW SUIT. The Irishman climbed and immediately was shown a number of shoddy garments by Spiegal, the eager salesman. Dugan refused to bite.

Spiegal knew that Zimmer, the boss, was watching him, so he made a special effort with the next number. Spiegal whirled the customer around and around before the mirror, crying, "It fits like a glove! You look like a movie star!"

When the Irishman again said "No," Zimmer took over, produced one blue serge suit, and made the sale in 5 minutes. As Dugan left, the boss said, "You see how easy it is when you know how? He went for the first suit I showed him."

"Yeah," agreed Spiegal, "but who made him dizzy?"

Edwin Lehman, Ship 'n Shore's dashing West Coast manager, delivers this delightful dash of drollery:

A sign in a Brooklyn candy store read: CIGARETTES 60 CENTS A PACKAGE. By 8:00 in the morning a line had already formed all around the block. Markowitz pushed his way to the front of the line.

Polowski, a big burly steelworker grabbed him and shouted, "Get to the rear of the line."

A few minutes later, Markowitz pushed his way through the crowd, got to the door, and the big Polack shoved him away.

Markowitz tried again, and again Polowski shoved him back. Finally, Markowitz said, "Look, if you push me, once more—I ain't gonna open the store!"

*"I ain't gonna open the store!"*

Sussman moved down South into one of the backwater towns and opened a general store. He seemed to be doing well, but then the beginning of April, sales started to slacken.

Sussman tried to figure out why business fell off. He walked down Main Street and discovered that every establishment had an Easter sign out front and that all the windows were especially dressed for the holiday.

Sussman was very religious—he couldn't very well acknowledge Easter. But he did work out the solution. That afternoon, Sussman's general store also had an Easter sign. It said:

CHRIST IS RISEN
BUT SUSSMAN'S PRICES
ARE STILL THE SAME

\* \* \*

Brodsky went to a house of ill repute. He paid $50 and relieved himself. When he finished, Gloria, his bedmate said, "That was great. You're the best I've had in a long time. If you want to go again, it's free."

Brodsky could not turn down such an offer. So he worked himself up, and once again released his pleasure.

When they finished, the girl said, "Mister, you're terrific! I enjoyed that so much that if you want to go again, I'll pay you $50!"

Brodsky rested 15 minutes, but no matter how hard he played with himself, it wouldn't stand up. Finally Brodsky gave up. He grabbed his putz and said, "You son-of-a-bitch bastard. When it comes to spending a buck, you're all there; but when it comes to make a dollar . . . !"

* * *

*Customer:* What do you mean! Seven hundred dollars for that antique! Last week you only wanted $450.

*Schulman:* Well, you know how the cost of labor and materials keeps going up.

39

Grobstein's Clothing Store stood on New York's Lower East Side. One day Grobstein went out for lunch and left Salter, his new salesman, in charge. When he came back Salter proudly announced, "I sold that black cloth coat."

"For how much?" asked Grobstein.

"Ninety-eight cents, like it said on the tag."

"Ninety-eight cents!" screamed the owner. "The tag said 98 *dollars*, you idiot!"

The clerk looked as if he would die of embarrassment. "Let this be a lesson to you!" said Grobstein, "but don't feel bad—we made 10¢ profit."

\* \* \*

## JEWISH FOOTBALL YELL

*Get that quarter back!*

\* \* \*

For 8 days and nights, Schlossberg the suit maker was unable to sleep. No medicine took effect and in desperation, the Schlossberg family brought in a famous hypnotist.

The hypnotist stared at Schlossberg and chanted, "You are asleep, Mr. Schlossberg. The shadows are closing about you. Soft music is lulling you into a state of lovely relaxation. You are asleep! You are asleep!"

"You're a miracle worker," sobbed the grateful son. He gave the hypnotist a big bonus and the man left in triumph.

As the outside door closed, Schlossberg opened one eye. "Say," he demanded, "is that shmuck gone yet?"

*     *     *

Sam and Irving owned a clothing store. When Sam returned from vacation, he was horrified to find his partner bandaged from head to toe, walking on crutches.

"What happened?" he asked.

"You remember the purple and green checked suit with the narrow lapels we've been stuck with for years?" said Irving. "I sold it!"

"So, what happened to you? The customer didn't like the suit?"

"The customer loved the suit," said Irving, "but the seeing eye dog nearly killed me!"

# YOU SHOULD LIVE THAT LONG

Old man Krastenfeld lay on his death-bed for months and finally passed away.

Two weeks later, the relatives gathered like vultures to hear the reading of the will.

The lawyer tore open an envelope, drew out a piece of paper and read:

"Being of sound mind, I spent every dime before I died."

\* \* \*

A Jewish woman in the Bronx recently caused quite a commotion by revealing the contents of her will. First, she stipulated that she be cremated. Then, she asked that her ashes be spread over Bloomingdale's so she'd be assured of having her daughter visit her at least twice a week.

Mrs. Moskowitz loved chicken soup. One evening she was spooning it up when three of her husband's friends came in. "Mrs. Moskowitz," the spokesman said, "we are here to tell you that your husband Izzy has been killed in an automobile accident."

Mrs. Moskowitz continued eating her soup. Again they told her. Still no reaction.

"Look," said the puzzled speaker, "we are telling you that your husband is dead."

She went right on with the soup. "Gentlemen," she said between mouthfuls, "soon as I'm finished with this chicken soup, you gonna hear some scream!"

*　*　*

Krebs was killed in an accident and Silverman was sent to break the news to his wife.

"Be careful how you tell her," advised a friend. "She's a very delicate woman!"

He knocked on the door and she came out. "Pardon me, are you the widow Krebs?"

"Certainly not."

"You wanna bet?"

Two members of the Shalom Retirement Home, Blustein and Levin, were strolling past the home of Nelson Rockefeller.

"If I only had that man's millions," sighed Bluestein, "I'd be richer than he is."

"Don't be a dummy," said Levin. "If you had his millions, you'd be as rich as he is—not any richer."

"You're wrong," said Blustein. "Don't forget—I could give Hebrew lessons on the side."

\* \* \*

A wealthy widower and his daughter were traveling to Europe on the S.S. *United States*. The girl fell overboard. Berman, aged 73, hit the water and saved her. After the two were brought back aboard the ship, the widower threw his arms around Berman.

"You saved my daughter's life," he exclaimed. "I'm a rich man. I'll give you anything. Ask me for whatever you want!"

"Just answer me one question!" said Berman. "Who pushed me?"

Nothing impressed Tannenbaum. When he watched Rod Carew get 5 hits against the Yankees, Tannenbaum commented, "It was okay." Even Muhammad Ali could not stir Tannenbaum to say more than, "He's all right!"

One night his wife dragged him to the circus. Act after act came on, and Tannenbaum sneered at each one.

Finally the M.C. introduced the main attraction. A man climbed to the top of the ladder, tiptoed out on a thin wire, and stood there. Then he balanced a lighted candle on his nose, and another one on his left foot. He took out a violin and put it under his chin. And then, suspended 200 feet above the gasping crowd, he began to play the overture from *Carmen*.

"Well," said Mrs. Tannenbaum, "what do you think of that?"

"So?" said Tannenbaum. "Heifetz he ain't!"

*"A Heifetz he ain't!"*

Eighty-year-old Hochman hobbled into his nephew Sheldon's new drugstore on the Lower East Side. "Hello, Uncle," he said, "we'll talk inside; I have to make a urinalysis." And he led the old man into the back room.

Hochman followed his nephew to the rear of the drugstore and found himself standing before the latest scientific equipment.

"How many urines you do a day?" asked Hochman.

"I'd say about 50," answered Sheldon.

"Fifty urines a day!" said the old man, "That's wonderful! When you finish, wash your hands and make me a malted!"

\* \* \*

Three grandmothers, Jacobson, Feldman, and Schwartz, met at a senior citizen get-together in Miami Beach. After nodding hello they got down to some real visiting.

"My son," said Mrs. Jacobson, "is a CPA and he sends me $300 a month."

"That's nice," offered Mrs. Feldman. "My son is a lawyer and he sends me $500 a month."

"Ladies," interjected Mrs. Schwartz,

"you don't know nothin' from having a good son. My boy is a veterinarian and he sends me $3000 a month."

" 'Scuse me, sweetheart," said Mrs. Jacobson. "$3000? How could a veterinarian make that kind of money?"

"Well," explained Mrs. Schwartz, "he owns a cat house in Baltimore, a cat house in Pittsburgh . . ."

\* \* \*

Seymour Grand, New Jersey's grandiloquent sandwich gourmet, provides customers with this gift of humor:

Sokolow, aged 75, rushed into a doctor's office. "You gotta give me a shot, so I should be young again," he pleaded. "I got a date with a young chicken tonight!"

"Just a minute," said the physician, "you're 75 years old. There's nothing I can do for you!"

"But doctor," exclaimed the old man, "my friend, Rosen, is 85, and he says he has sex three times a week!"

"All right," advised the doctor, "so you *say* it too!"

Marty Sinaisky, California's most charming gynecologist, came up with this cutie:

On a Tuesday afternoon at 1:00, an elderly Jewish couple came to Dr. Berger's office and asked him to witness their sexual technique. He did and told them that they were normal.

They paid his $20 fee, but came back again the following week, and the week after that.

After the 6th demonstration, the doctor said, "You two are not only normal but very good partners. Why do you keep coming back?"

The man replied, "Well, Doc, this kind of thing ain't covered by Medicare and at $20 a visit, you're cheaper than a motel!"

\* \* \*

Gene Gach, the personable Vista Del Mar public relations director, gets guffaws on this great gag:

Lieberman was standing at the edge of the ocean on Miami Beach when he recognized Mrs. Gross, a woman from his neighborhood. "Hello," he said, "you're here without your husband."

"Yeah," she replied. "He couldn't leave the store."

"Listen, Mrs. Gross, could I be perfectly honest with you?"

"Why not? Don't I know you from the neighborhood 30 years?"

"My dear Mrs. Gross, I have admired you from the distance for a long time. You are a lovely woman. I always wanted to have a little something with you. Why don't you come with me up to my hotel room and we could have some terrific good time."

"Say," answered the surprised woman, "let's move into the water. People can see what we're talkin' about."

*   *   *

Janowitz was living it up at a Ft. Lauderdale senior citizens dance and he lost his wallet containing $600. "Excuse me," he announced, standing on a chair, "but I lost my wallet with $600 in it. To the man that finds it I will give $50."

A voice from the rear shouted, "I'll give $75."

During the 50th year of their marriage, the Teitelbergs won a big prize in the state lottery and bought a house in the country. Mrs. Teitelberg was showing off their estate to a visiting poor relation from the city.

"Mrs. Teitelberg," asked the visitor as they looked at the poultry, "do your hens lay eggs?"

"Yes," said Mrs. Teitelberg, "but they don't have to. We can afford to buy them now."

\* \* \*

The lawyer stood before the family of the recently deceased Hershel Ostrow and read aloud his will:

"To my dear wife, I leave my house, 50 acres of land and one million dollars."

"To my son, Rubie, I leave my two cars and $200,000."

"To my daughter, Sarah, I leave my yacht and $200,000."

"And to my brother-in-law, who always insisted that health is better than wealth, I leave my sun lamp."

# MY SON, THE DOCTOR

Siegel went to an optician and announced, "I want to get my eyes tested for a pair of glasses."

The doctor placed him in front of a card and asked, "Can you read that plainly?"

"No, I can't," replied Siegel.

The doctor moved the card closer and asked, "Can you read it now?"

"No, I can't."

The doctor took the card and pushed it right under his nose. "Well, can you read it now?"

"No," said Siegel. "I never learned to read yet."

The phone rang at the nurse's desk on the 5th floor at Mt. Sinai Hospital. "Nurse, can you tell me how Mr. Kaminsky is getting along?"

"Just fine," said the nurse, looking at her charts. "Doctor says he can go home on Thursday. Who shall I say called him?"

"No one. I'm Kaminsky. That doctor treats me like an idiot—he won't tell me nothin' !"

\* \* \*

"All Jewish baby boys are born the same size," said the doctor.

"What size?" asked the medical student.

"Circumcize," answered the doctor smiling.

\* \* \*

"She had teeth just like pearls."

"That's not surprising. She and Pearl go to the same dentist."

"*Help! My son Morris the doctor,
whose office is at 520 Park Avenue,
is drowning!*"

Jack Foreman, the leading Alfa Romeo dealer in the West, loves this looney:

At a dentist's office one day, Mrs. Glucksman was arguing over her bill. The charge for an inlay was $100. "Couldn't you make it $90?" she protested.

The rest of the bill came to $150. The woman asked, "Couldn't you make it $130?"

Finally, Mrs. Glucksman asked what time the dentist expected her the following morning.

"Eleven o'clock," he said.

A patient in the waiting room shouted, "Can't you make it ten-thirty?"

\* \* \*

Rutkin and Sakolsky were walking home from a lodge meeting.

"So what is your son doing for a living?" asked Rutkin.

"He got some crazy idea in college. He studied to be a psychiatrist."

"So how is he doing?"

"Not bad!"

"Why not?" answered Sakolsky. "I understand these fellers pick up plenty of change that falls behind the couch!"

In a crowded theatre, Mrs. Bleiberg tripped and fell down the stairs. Moaning in pain, she screamed, "Is there a doctor in the house?"

Finally, a tall, handsome young man came over and said, "Yes, Madam, I'm a doctor."

"Oh, Doctor," wailed Mrs. Bleiberg. "Have I got a lovely daughter for you!"

*　　*　　*

Joyce Goldberg, the bubbling better half of Joyce Bertram, Houston's best bath boutique, brightens up Texas with this bauble:

Fenton's wife was going to have a baby and he couldn't get a doctor. The snow outside was 8 feet deep, the telephone lines were down, and it was still snowing. He decided to go out and look for an M.D.

He fought his way through the storm and saw a light which turned out to be a bar. He went in and began drinking heavily.

"What's the matter?" said Hymowitz, sitting on a nearby stool.

"My wife is going to have a baby," cried Fenton, "and I can't find a doctor..."

"I can help you," said the Jewish man.

(con't)

(Con't from page 57)

"Are you a doctor?"

"I'm a veterinarian. But you gimme your address, I'll go get my satchel, and I'll come over and do the job for you."

Fenton rushed home and soon Hymowitz arrived carrying his satchel.

"Now don't worry about a thing," he said. "Get blankets, plenty of hot water." He went into the bedroom.

Twenty minutes, Hymowitz came out, sweat pouring from his brow and said, "You got a hammer?"

"A hammer?" roared Fenton. "What do you want it for?"

"Don't ask no questions, get me a hammer."

Fenton brought him the tool and Hymowitz said, "Don't worry about nothin'. Get plenty hot water, lots of blankets!" He ran back into the bedroom.

Thirty minutes later he came out, stripped to the waist, perspiration pouring from his body. He said, "Hey, you got a chisel?"

"My God!" screamed Fenton. "First you want a hammer. Now it's a chisel. What are you doing to my wife?"

"What do you mean, your *wife?* First I gotta open the satchel!"

*"First, I gotta open my satchel!"*

Michael Paige, California's foremost convention show producer, perks up clients with this pleasureful pleaser:

At a crowded cocktail party of Long Island, Mrs. Rosenbaum was introduced to Dr. Weinberg.

"Oh, Doctor," she wailed, "I'm so glad to meet you. You see, I have this little problem. Every time I raise my right arm, I get this funny little pain in my side."

"I am sorry," said Dr. Weinberg, "but I'm afraid I can't help you. I happen to be a doctor of economics."

"In that case," said Mrs. Rosenbaum, "tell me, should I sell my Polaroid shares?"

\* \* \*

Mrs. Schoenfeld was very jealous because all her neighbors were getting things free from Medicare. One had new teeth, another had new glasses, and when the woman next door got a free hearing aid, it was the last straw.

She went to the doctor and said, "I'd like to cut a hole in my stomach."

"Ah, I see, your husband is not satisfied

with the one you've got, and you want me to make you a new one?"

"Oh, no, I want you to make a hole and fit a piece of glass in it."

"Mrs. Schoenfeld, I'll prescribe some tranquilizers."

"I don't want tranquilizers!"

"What do you want then?"

"I've just told you—a womb with a view!"

# MATRIMONIAL MISHMASH

Budnick had a fight with his wife, and went to the Turkish baths to steam out. Later in the evening he decided to phone home and maybe apologize. So he called her up.

"Hello, sweetie," he said. "What are you makin' for dinner?"

"What I'm makin', you bum? Poison, that's what I'm makin'. Poison!"

"So make only one portion! I'm not comin' home."

\* \* \*

"I'd divorce Milton in a minute," Mrs. Cooper told the woman doing her hair.

"Then why don't you?" asked the beautician.

"Because it would kill me to see him so happy."

L. Jason Seale, Trenton's top-notch CPA, tells this tidy titillator:

When Weissberg got married he said to his wife, "Every time we make love, I'm gonna give you a dollar bill!"

And true to his word, each time Weissberg boffed his bride, he gave her a buck, which she promptly deposited in a wooden box. Then Weissberg had to go on a business trip. He took his spouse's picture with him and every time he dreamed of making love to her, he mailed her a dollar.

"Darling," said Weissberg when he arrived home, "let's see how much we saved in the box!"

They opened it and out fell $5, $10, and $20 bills. "How's this possible?" asked Weissberg. "I only gave you a dollar at a time!"

"Yes, darling," said his wife. "But other men ain't as stingy as you!"

\* \* \*

## MRS. PONCE DE LEON TO HER HUSBAND:
*"Like hell you're gonna go to Miami without me!"*

On her deathbed, Beatrice was giving final instructions to her husband.

"Eli, you've been so good to me all these years. I know you never even thought about another woman. Now that I'm going, I want you to marry again as soon as possible, and I want you to give your new wife all my expensive clothes."

"I can't do that, darling," he said. "You're a size 16 and she's only a 10!"

*  *  *

The new neighbor joined the Mah-Jongg group for the first time, and all the ladies gaped at the huge diamond she wore. "It's the third most famous diamond in the world," she told the women. "First is the Cullinan diamond, then the Hope diamond, and then this one—the Horowitz diamond."

It's beautiful!" said Mrs. Fisch. "You're so lucky!"

"Not so lucky," sighed the newcomer. "Unfortunately, with the famous Horowitz diamond, I am afflicted with the famous Horowitz curse."

"What's that?" asked Mrs. Fisch.

"*Mr.* Horowitz," said the woman.

Tillie and Hilda got together for their usual morning cup of coffee.

"Did you meet that new woman who moved in across the street?" asked Tillie.

"I certainly did!" exclaimed Hilda. "She couldn't stop complaining about her husband."

"Believe me, there's nothin' worse than a complaining wife," said Tillie. "Now take me. My husband is a gambler, he drinks too much, he stays out late—a worse husband you never saw in your life. But do I ever say anything to anybody?"

\* \* \*

Gussie had lived a good life, having been married four times. Now she stood before the Pearly Gates.

Father Abraham said to her, "I notice that you first married a banker, then an actor, next a rabbi, and lastly an undertaker. What kind of a system is that for a respectable Jewish woman?"

"A very good system," replied Gussie, "One for the money, two for the show, three to make ready and four to go!"

Jack Novack, California's super celebrity caterer, contributed this kooky convulser:

A woman at the grave of her husband was wailing, "Oh, Joseph, it's four years since you've gone but I still miss you!"

Just then Grosberg passed by and saw the woman crying. " 'Scuse me," he said, "who are you mourning?"

"My husband," she said. "I miss him so much."

Grosberg looked at the stone and then said, "Your husband? But it says on the gravestone: SACRED TO THE MEMORY OF GOLDA KREPS."

"Oh, yes, he put everything in my name."

*"Everything's in my name."*

"Is it true, Max, that your mother-in-law is ill?"

"Yes."

"In fact, I hear she is in the hospital?"

"Yes."

"How long has she been in the hospital?"

"In three weeks time, please God, it will be a month."

\* \* \*

Mrs. Muchnik was still recovering after having a baby. She gave her husband $20 from under her pillow to go to a bawdy house and not bother her. On the way he met Goldie, the woman who lived downstairs.

"Why go to strangers?" she said, "I'll do the same thing for you even better."

He returned home early, explaining what happened to his wife.

"Then give me back the $20."

"Oh, I gave that to Goldie downstairs," said the husband, "she asked for it."

"The nerve!" screamed his wife. "When she had her second baby, I didn't ask her husband for a dime!"

The Gottliebs were celebrating their 25th anniversary at Grossinger's with the biggest party held there in years. The husband sat at the head table totally depressed. His lawyer walked over to him and said, "What's wrong? Why do you look so unhappy?"

"Do you remember on my fifth anniversary," said Gottlieb, "I asked you what would happen if I murdered my wife?"

"Yes," answered the attorney, "I told you you'd get 20 years!"

"You see," said Gottlieb, "tonight, I'd be a free man!"

\* \* \*

Rosenbloom was all bandaged and on crutches. "What happened?" asked Greenfield.

"I was in a train accident. I collected $50,000 and my wife collected $20,-000."

"Oh," said Greenfield, "your wife was hurt, too?"

"Not from the wreck," replied Rosenbloom. "In the excitement I had the presence of mind to give her a good kick in the face."

Jack Solomon, Keansburg's favorite son, saves this special saga for his sophisticated buddies:

Moe and Sophie had been married for 12 years. One night in bed Moe said, "Lift up the nightgown."

Sophie didn't answer.

Moe tried once again. "Hey, be a good girl. Lift up the nightgown."

Sophie still didn't reply.

Moe stormed out of the room, slamming the door. Sophie got up and locked it.

For half an hour, Moe walked the living room. Then he strode back to the bedroom, pushed on the door, and found it was locked.

"Open the door," he pleaded, "I'm sorry I got sore. Open the door."

Sophie didn't answer.

"If you don't open the door, I'll break it down!"

"Look at my athlete!" shouted Sophie. "A nightgown he can't lift up, but a door he'll break down!"

\* \* \*

Marty Wogansky, the Main Showroom's merry maître d' at Atlantic City's Resorts

International Hotel, makes monkeyshines with this magnificent fable:

Only in America could this heart-warming story take place: A Jewish boy was born on the Lower East Side of New York of poverty-stricken immigrant parents. He grew up, married a neighborhood girl, and had several children. For years he struggled, then all of a sudden his luck changed. He became tremendously wealthy. He owned steel mills, oil refineries, railroads. He had a home in Palm Springs, a villa in Spain, an estate in Rome. But he never forgot.

Every year he goes back to the Lower East Side, just to visit his wife and children.

\* \* \*

Hershkowitz bragged about his wife's unusual beauty. "You mean," said a friend, "that you don't know that your wife has four lovers?"

"Well," said Hershkowitz, "I'd rather have a 20-percent interest in a good deal than a 100-percent interest in a bad one."

Mrs. Ashkenazy loved concerts. Her husband hated them. One night he did everything possible to be late for a performance at the Music Center.

They finally arrived at 10:00. The orchestra was in the middle of an opus. Mrs. Ashkenazy looked at the program and said, "We are now into Beethoven's Ninth Symphony."

"Oh, boy," said her husband, "am I glad I missed the other eight."

\* \* \*

"Another new dress?" screamed Eisenberg. "Where am I gonna get the money to pay for it all?"

"I may be a lot of things," said Mrs. Eisenberg, "but inquisitive, I'm not!"

# A SHAME FOR THE NEIGHBORS

Yetta and Lillian met in front of their Bronx tenement.

"Oh, my," exclaimed Yetta. "Do you hear what's going on in the Middle East, Portugal, and Spain?"

"I don't see nothin'," said Lillian. "I live in the back of the building."

\* \* \*

Mrs. Ganz called Mrs. Slutsky to the dumbwaiter to get some advice about what movie she should see with her husband that night.

"How's the picture at the Lowies?" she asked. "Any good?"

"Don't go!" shouted Mrs. Slutsky. "We walked out in the middle. It was impossible to sit through it twice!"

Two women met totally naked in a Turkish bath.

"Hello, Mrs. Halpern, how are you?"

The second woman didn't answer.

"Mrs. Halpern, don't you recognize me?"

"You look very familiar."

"I'm your next door neighbor!"

"Oh, I didn't recognize you without the glasses!"

\* \* \*

Plotkie the plumber died. His union called a meeting to raise money for his bereft wife and children. Contributions were to be voluntary.

The union president made an emotional speech and soon the men started to weep and sob out loud. There wasn't a dry eye in the hall.

But Goldberg sat there unmoved, not a trace of emotion showing on his face. His neighbor turned to him and said, "How come you're not crying?"

"I'm not a member here," replied Goldberg.

Barbi Fleigleman was sent to the finest finishing school in Connecticut. At her mother's insistence she majored in etiquette and four years later received her degree.

One night, a few months after graduation, Barbi walked into the Fliegelman flat in the Bronx and announced, "I'm pregnant!"

"You know who the father is?" asked Mrs. Fliegelman.

"No, I don't."

"You mean after all the etiquette you studied you didn't even ask, 'With whom am I having the pleasure?' "

\* \* \*

My friend Mimi Marks, of New Jersey, manufactured this mirthful marvel:

Mrs. Bornstein unexpectedly bumped into Mrs. Freeman in the lobby of New York's Plaza Hotel.

"Shhh," said Mrs. Bornstein, "Don't tell anybody, I'm having an affair."

"Oh," said Mrs. Freeman, "and who's gonna be the caterer?"

| | |
|---|---|
| *Newman:* | Have you traveled much? |
| *Bender:* | Yeah, last summer I took a trip down the Mississippi. |
| *Newman:* | Did you see the levees? |
| *Bender:* | Naw, they were away. We stopped with the Cohens. |

\* \* \*

"Did you see the movie, *Jaws*?"

"What a question. Of course."

"Did you see *Jaws Two*?"

"Naturally."

"Well, don't miss the sequel. It's called *Jews* and it's about loan sharks."

\* \* \*

Adler and Saperstein were traveling out West in a stagecoach when, without warning, they were held up by highwaymen.

Saperstein immediately pulled out a roll of bills from his pocket. "Adler," he said, "here's that fifty dollars I owe you."

Adele Khoury, Hollywood's top voice teacher, tells students this titanic tidbit:

Three women sitting on the West Hampton beach got into a conversation, "My name is Epstein," said one, "I have a mink stole, my husband earns $75,000 a year and every winter we go to Miami Beach!"

"My name is Zeitlin," said the second. "I have a full length mink coat, my husband earns $100,000 a year and every winter we travel around the world!"

"My name is Liebowitz," said the third. "We own a little candy store in Brooklyn and some years when business is good we make $4000. I own a cloth coat and I never had a vacation in my life!"

Mrs. Epstein tapped Mrs. Zeitlin and said, "Tell me, sweetheart, isn't Liebowitz a Puerto Rican name?"

\* \* \*

**JEWISH-MEXICAN RESTAURANT**
*Casa Hadassah*

The Bravermans married off their last daughter and decided to sell their house and move into a furnished apartment.

Mr. Braverman showed his wife the apartment he rented.

"I don't like it," said Mrs. Braverman.

"Why not?" asked Mr. Braverman.

"There's no curtains in the bathroom. Every time I take a bath, the neighbors'll be able to see me in the nude!"

"Don't worry," said her husband, "when the neighbors see you in the nude they'll buy the curtains!"

"When they see you nude,
they'll buy the curtains!"

After a performance at a Miami condominium an elderly man walked up to the great entertainer, Mickey Katz.

" 'Scuse me, Mr. Katz," said the senior citizen, "ain't your son Joel Grey?"

"Yes," replied Mickey proudly.

"What was his name before?"

"Katz."

"Yeah. I knew he was a Jewish boy!"

\* \* \*

"Hello! This is long distance. I have a call for you from Palm Springs."

"Hello, Herman, this is Rube. Listen, I'm stranded here and I need $500."

"I can't hear you. Something is wrong with the phone."

"*I want $500.*"

"I still can't hear you."

"I can hear it okay," interrupted the operator.

"Then *you* give him the $500."

Hogarty was talking to Abrams. "How is it that Jews are so smart?" asked the Irishman.

"Because," said Abrams, "we eat a certain kind of fish. Here, I'll sell you this one for twenty dollars."

Hogarty paid his money and after receiving a small dried fish, he bit into it. "Why," exclaimed the son of Erin, "this is only a smoked herring."

"See?" said Abrams, "you're gettin' smart already."

*　*　*

One morning, Weintraub went to a restaurant and ordered bacon with his eggs. He was an orthodox Jew and his wife kept a strictly kosher home. But Weintraub felt the need just this once.

As Weintraub was about to leave the restaurant, he stopped in the door, frozen with terror. The sky was filled with black clouds, there was lightning, and the ground shook with the rumble of thunder.

"Can you imagine!" he exclaimed. "All that fuss over a little piece of bacon!"

At breakfast, Feinberg's wife said to him, "We're having Sonia's boyfriend to dinner for the first time. We're gonna have a big meal with our best dishes. So please behave. Don't eat with your knife, or you'll kill her chance for marriage." Feinberg agreed.

That night at supper all went well. Feinberg hardly touched a thing for fear of using the wrong tool. Then coffee arrived. Feinberg took the cup and started to pour his java into the saucer. The family was looking daggers at him. Feinberg kept right on pouring. Finally, the saucer was full.

Feinberg raised it to his mouth, looked around the table, and said, "One word out of any of you, and I'll make bubbles!"

*"I'll make bubbles!"*

"What are you crying for, Mr. Mendel? Is the rich man who just died a relative of yours?"

"No, he ain't. That's why I'm crying!"

\* \* \*

*The first mink said, "You'll never guess what my husband is getting me for Christmas!"*
*"What?" asked the second mink.*
*"A full length Jew!"*

\* \* \*

Chislov went to a Catskill hotel with one objective: He was going to eat everything he could. *Why not?* he told himself. *Ain't I paying for it?* The first morning he said to the waitress, "At every meal I want you to bring me *two* of everything."

For breakfast Chislov had two grapefruits, two plates of prunes, two cereals, two of everything. Lunch and dinner were the same. On his last day he had a dinner of two soups, two plates of bread, two helpings of roast beef, with double orders of noodles, corn and baked potatoes on the side, two Waldorf salads, two pots of coffee and two slices of apricot pie. By now, his blood pressure was rising so rapidly that, just as he got the last forkful down, he toppled over onto the floor.

The busboy, the waitress and the maître d' ran to his side. They opened his collar and fanned him, and then the manager rushed up with a glass of water.

Chislov slowly opened his eyes, "What's with the water?" he said. "Bring me two malted milks."

# ORTHODOX, CONSERVATIVE AND REFORMED

"God must be Jewish," one famous theologian finally admitted. "Who else would have worked a six-day week?"

\* \* \*

A rabbi's son converted to Christianity and the clergyman was totally distraught. God himself came down to earth to console him. "After all," said the Lord, "didn't the same thing happen to My son 2000 years ago?"

"Yes," replied the rabbi, "but don't forget, my son was legitimate."

Young Goldstein was a long Island phenomenon. He not only graduated from high school as valedictorian, but he established all kinds of passing records as New York's finest football player. Goldstein elected to go to Notre Dame. When he came home for his first vacation, his rabbi, who wasn't too happy about the whole procedure, asked anxiously, "My boy, they aren't Catholicizing you there at South Bend, are they?"

The youth replied, "I should say not, Father."

\* \* \*

Garfunkel and Levine met after Sabbath services. "Our rabbi is such a good man," said Garfunkel. "He lives very sparingly on his meager salary; and he won't accept payment for any special services he performs for any member of the congregation. He won't even accept a gratuity for performing a marriage."

"Yes," agreed Levine, "as a matter of fact, the man would probably starve to death except for one thing: Every Monday and Thursday he fasts!"

# YOM KIPPUR

## *Instant Lent*

\* \* \*

Donna Corwin, the sophisticated Scarsdale student, cracks up school chums with this silly:

Rabbi Miller said to 6-year-old Jerome, "So your mother says your prayers for you each night?"

"Yes, sir," answered the boy.

"Very commendable. What does she say?"

"Thank God he's in bed!" replied Jerome.

\* \* \*

Little Shirley swallowed a penny.

"Quick," shouted the child's mother. "Call the doctor!"

"Doctor, nothing!" yelled the father. "Send for the rabbi. That guy can get money out of anybody!"

The synagogue was holding a raffle to raise money for a new building. The third prize winner was announced and he won a beautiful color television set. Then they announced the second prize winner. It was Smulowitz. He walked up to collect his prize—a sponge cake.

"A sponge cake!" shouted Smulowitz to the man beside him. "Who wants a sponge cake? I spent $100 on a raffle ticket, third prize is a color TV and I win a sponge cake? I ain't gonna take a sponge cake!"

"Shhh," said the man. "The sponge cake was baked by the rabbi's wife."

"Screw the rabbi's wife," said Smulowitz.

"Sssshhh," said the man, "that's the first prize!"

\* \* \*

Harper was sitting on a train between a rabbi and a priest. After an hour of banal comments, Harper said, "Ah, the Old and the New Testament."

"Yes," said the rabbi, "and the space between them is usually completely blank."

"It won't be long now!" said the rabbi as he circumcised the little boy.

*   *   *

The Silversteins sent their son to a high-brow New England boarding school. A few months later he returned home for the Christmas holidays.

"Samela," greeted his mother. "It's so good to see you."

"Mother," he replied, "stop calling me Samela. I'm grown up now and I wish you would refer to me as Samuel."

"I'm sorry," said Mrs. Silverstein. "I hope you ate only kosher foods while you were away?"

"Mother, it's ridiculous to still cling to those old world traditions. I indulged in all types of food, kosher and non-kosher, and you would be better off if you did."

"Well, did you at least go to the synagogue occasionally?"

"Really!" replied the young Silverstein. "Going to a synagogue when you're associating with mostly non-Jews is preposterous. It's unfair to ask it of me."

"Tell me, son," said Mrs. Silverstein, "are you still circumcised?"

What happened in A.D. 13?
Jesus was bar mitzvahed.

*   *   *

Three reformed and very progressive rabbis were boasting about the advanced views of their respective congregations.

"We're so modern," said the first, "we've installed ashtrays in every pew so members can smoke while they meditate."

"Ah," snorted the second. "We now have a snack bar in the basement that serves ham sandwiches after services."

"You boys," said the third, "aren't even in the same class with *my* congregation. We're so reformed we close for the Jewish holidays!"

*   *   *

"The new cantor of our temple is certainly great. What a beautiful singing voice!"

"Eh, if I had a voice like his, I'd sing just as good!"

Joseph Amega, proprietor of Princess Ermine Jewels, California's finest gem dispensers, picked up this pleasant piece of persiflage:

In a southern city a Catholic church and a synagogue stood side by side.

Rabbi Bomberg and Father Sheehan were good friends.

Unfortunately they got into a competition. When the priest's parishioners bought him a Buick, Rabbi Bomberg had the congregation buy him a Cadillac.

The following morning, Father Sheehan went out with holy water and baptized his car. Before he was finished Rabbi Bomberg came dashing out with a plumber's shears and cut three inches off his own car's exhaust pipe.

Sydenberg had lived a virtuous life. He was even president of the synagogue. But when he entered Heaven, the angel in charge said, "You can't stay here."

"Why?" asked Sydenberg. "I always tried to be a good man."

"That's it," explained the angel. "Everyone here was a good man but they all committed at least *one* sin. Since you didn't sin at all, the rest of the souls will resent you."

"But," protested Sydenberg, "isn't there something I can do?"

"Well," considered the angel, "you can have six more hours on earth to commit a sin, but you must do somebody a real injury."

Sydenberg went back to earth and suddenly he saw a middle-aged woman looking at him. They started talking. She invited him home with her. Soon they were making love like two teenagers.

Six hours later Sydenberg said, "I'm sorry but I have to go now."

"Listen," cried the woman. "I never married or even had a man. You just gave me the best time I had in my whole life! What a good deed you did today!"

Rabinowitz went to his rabbi and moaned, "I'm in terrible trouble. I can't support my wife and seven children, and every year there comes still another baby. What should I do?"

"Don't do anything at all," advised the rabbi.

\* \* \*

Mrs. Weissman lived in the 30th-floor penthouse of her Park Avenue building. Every day when she went up or down in the elevator, Manelli the elevator man would see her making the sign of the cross. After watching this for several days he couldn't resist asking her if she was Catholic. She replied, "Definitely not, I'm Jewish."

"I no understand," said Manelli. "If you Jewish why you cross yourself every time you get in and out of the elevator?"

"Cross myself!" barked Mrs. Weissman. "Don't be ridiculous! I'm checking to see if I have my tiara, my brooch, my clip . . . *my clip!!!*"

Clancy and Greenberg were bragging about their heritage. "One of my ancestors," claimed Clancy, "signed the Declaration of Independence."

"Really?" replied Greenberg, "one of mine signed the Ten Commandments."

\* \* \*

Perlman made millions in the bakery business. While on a visit to Rome, he went to see the Pope and made a huge donation to the Church.

The Pope was very pleased and said, "Mr. Perlman, is there anything I can do to show my appreciation?"

"Yes, Your Holiness," answered the baking magnate. "Could you make a little change in the Lord's Prayer?"

"Oh, Mr. Perlman," frowned the Pope, "I'm afraid that wouldn't be possible. The Lord's Prayer is repeated daily by millions of Christians."

"I know," said Perlman, "but I only want a small change. Where it says, 'Give us this day our daily bread,' just make it, 'Give us this day Perlman's pumpernickel bread.'"

Flaherty and Gluckstein were discussing the merits of their religion. "Answer me this," said the Irishman, "could one of your boys be Pope?"

"No," answered Gluckstein. "Could one of your boys be God?"

"Why, of course not!" replied Flaherty.

"Well," said Gluckstein, "one of our boys made it."

*　*　*

Who was the only happy Jewish mother?

Jesus' mother.

*　*　*

Alan, a real ladies man, rushed into a Catholic church. He slipped into the confession booth and said, "Father, Father, I just made love to a woman 25 times!"

"Are you married?" asked the priest.

"No," said Alan, "and I'm Jewish, not Catholic, but I had to tell someone!"

# ELEVEN O'CLOCK MASS

The snow was blowing out of doors,
The drifts were piling high,
And I could see pedestrians
As they were passing by.

The faces of all my Irish friends
Came dimly thru the glass
As they trudged the icy streets
To worship at their Mass.

I watched awhile, went back to bed
And cuddled safe and sound
As they braced those icy blasts
On sacred duty bound.

I envy them their strength of heart
The faith that they renew,
But on this ice-cold Sunday morn
It's good to be a Jew.

\* \* \*

# Best-Selling Sports Books
# from Pinnacle

## SAINTS BE PRAISED!

More ethnic hilarity from the
world's best-selling humorist!

*　　*　　*

"That was a beautiful hat your wife
wore to church this morning," remarked
Gannon. "It was so high I could hardly see
the pulpit above it."

"It should'a been beautiful," replied
Gannon. "An' if she'd worn the bill that
come with it, you wouldn't a seen the
steeple!"

*　　*　　*

MORE

The Official Irish Joke Book

BY Larry Wilde

PINNACLE BOOKS • LOS ANGELES

MORE

The Official Irish Joke Book

# Contents

# SONS OF ERIN

An English clergyman turned to Angus MacDuff and asked him, "What would you be were you not a Scot?"

"Why an Englishman, of course," said the Scotsman.

Then the clergyman turned to Dennehy and asked him, "And what would you be were you not an Irishman?"

"Why," said Dennehy, "I'd be ashamed of meself!"

*   *   *

A stranger stopped an Irishman in New Jersey. "Say, Pat, how far is it to Newark?"

"How did ye know my name?"

"I guessed it."

"Then guess how far it is to Newark."

3

O'Keefe and MacNally went into the fancy restaurant and ordered the deluxe dinner with all the trimmings. Then O'Keefe called for the manager.

"There's a fly in my soup," he said to him. "This is terrible. I never expected anything like this to happen in such a fine place."

"Ssh," pleaded the manager, "not so loud. I'm really sorry. Gentlemen, there will be no check. Dinner is on the house."

When they finished, the two men left and O'Keefe pointed to a drugstore across the street. "Could you go for an ice cream soda?" he asked MacNally. "I've got one more fly left."

\*     \*     \*

### IRISH FOLK SONG

*McCarthy is dead and McGuinness don't know it.*
*McGuinness is dead and McCarthy don't know it .*
*They both are dead in the very same bed,*
*And neither one knows that the other is dead.*

# IRISH DIP

*A roll in the hay*

\* \* \*

Eugene O'Neill, the great American-Irish playright, didn't pay much attention to critics, but there was one piece of advice he took without question. After the premiere of "The Hairy Ape," to which O'Neill had invited a lot of his seafaring friends, one of the sailors came up to him.

"Gene," he said. "I think the show's terrific—but for God's sake tell that Number Four stoker to stop leaning his butt against that red-hot furnace."

\* \* \*

Healy was working as a doorman at a very fine New York Hotel. One night a man failed to tip Healy, and he said to him, "If you happen to lose your wallet on the way home, sir, remember, you didn't pull it out here."

"Colleen, did I see you kissing that policeman in the kitchen? I'm amazed at you!"

"Well, mum, it's against the law to resist an officer."

*　*　*

Killoran was considered by most of the villagers to be the dumbest man in the town. One day he showed up in new clothes and began buying rounds of drinks at the neighborhood saloon. The neighbors wondered what had happened.

When one of them finally asked him, Killoran replied, "I won the first prize in the big lottery."

"How'd you ever guess the lucky number?"

"Well, three times running I dreamed of seven. So I figured it out that three times seven is twenty-four, and I bought ticket number twenty-four, and it won."

"Why, you fool, three times seven is twenty-one, not twenty-four."

"You've got the education," said Killoran. "I've got the lottery money."

During World War I, when Harrigan was in France, his wife wrote to him. "There isn't an able-bodied man left in Ireland," she said, "and I'm gonna have to dig up the garden meself."

Harrigan wrote back. "Don't dig up the garden. That's where the guns are."

The letter was censored and soldiers came to the house and dug up every square foot of the garden. "I don't know what to do," wrote Mrs. Harrigan to her husband. "Soldiers came and dug up the whole garden."

Harrigan wrote back, "Now plant the potatoes."

\* \* \*

Mrs. Goldstein opened the door and found Leary the bum on the doorstep. "Please, me good woman, could you spare me a bit of creamy cake?"

"Now, wouldn't bread be much better for you?"

"I know, ma'am," said Leary. "But today's me birthday."

Trent Christman, guiding star of the Armed Forces radio in Frankfurt, tells this tidbit of tomfoolery:

McGuffy was working at a construction site on the outskirts of Boston.

The foreman loaded McGuffy's wheelbarrow to the sky with lead piping.

"I beg your pardon, sir," said the Irishman. "Would you mind tying a couple of concrete blocks to my ankles?"

"What for?"

"To stop me from breakin' into a run."

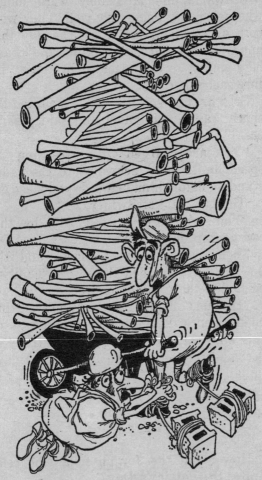

"*I might be breakin' into a run!*"

Schwartz and McSwiney were judges who never got along very well. They were both arrested for speeding. The day they appeared in court they found the chambers empty, so they decided to appear before each other.

Schwartz put on his cloak, mounted the bench, rapped his gavel and said, "First case!"

"You are charged with exceeding the speed limit," said Schwartz to the judge standing before him. "How do you plead?"

"Guilty!" said McSwiney.

"You are hereby fined $10 by this court. Step down, next case."

Then they exchanged places and the Jewish judge pleaded the same. "Guilty," he said to the speeding charge.

"Hmmm," said McSwiney now sitting on the bench. "This is the second case of this kind we've had this mornin'. They've become far too numerous. $20 or 10 days in jail!"

*   *   *

How about the Jewish fella who celebrates St. Patrick's Day?

His name is Aaron-Go bragh!

"How's yer rheumatism, John?"

"Ah, me rheumatism's thrivin' finely, Dobie. I'm the one that's gettin' the worst of it entirely."

\* \* \*

Eddie Rosen, Hollywood's popular movie producer, pleases pals with this pint of pleasure:

While working on the 9th floor of a building Fitzpatrick missed his footing and fell off a scaffold. He hit a telephone wire on the way down, whirled around, struck a clothes line, and landed in a pile of discarded hay from a packing case.

By a miracle Fitzpatrick was unhurt. As the Irishman came to, a paramedic was holding a glass of water to his lips.

"What the devil happened—did the building fall?"

"No, but you did. You had a very narrow escape from death."

"What's that ye're givin' me to drink?"

"Water, to revive you," answered the paramedic.

"Givin' me water after fallin' nine stories! Faith, an' how far would I have to fall to get a drink of whiskey?"

# GREETING CARD

*Happy St. Pat's Day!*
*May you be wearing green stains on your*
*shillelagh, from a roll in the shamrocks!*

❈   ❈   ❈

Egan won a bundle of money in the sweepstakes lottery, transforming him from a pauper to a wealthy man.

A reporter from the local newspaper checked on him a year later.

"Have you found, sir, that the money has changed you any?" asked the newshound.

"Well, for one thing," replied Egan, "I'm now eccentric where I used to be just plain crazy. And for another thing, I'm now clever and witty where I was once just the fellow who knew the punch lines to all the dirty jokes."

# SAME OLD SHILLELAGH

"Are you sober, O'Flaherty?"
"Yes, sir. Often."

\* \* \*

Kilkelly lurched up against Greenberg on the street and burped, "Shay, Mishter, what have I got in my right hand?"

"Nothing," said Greenberg.

"Then what'sh in my left hand?" asked Kilkelly.

"Nothing."

The Irishman groaned, "Oh, poo, I'm piddling in my pantsh again!"

"I've been drinkin' whiskey all week to cure my sciatica," admitted McNally.

"I can give you a cure."

"Shut up. I don't want to hear it."

\* \* \*

Salesman: I have something here that'll make you feel like a new man, bring new friendship and popularity into your life and . . .

Calhalane: Never mind the rest, I'll take a quart.

\* \* \*

Mrs. Muleen was arguing with her daughter Rose. "Tis a shame, that husband of yours," she exclaimed. "Never been seen without a bottle in his mouth!"

"That's not true, Momma!" protested Rose in her husband's defense. "Sometimes Archie stops drinking."

"To do what?" asked her mother.

"Well, to belch, for one!" replied Rose.

In Las Vegas, Devlin, sloshed to the gills, got into a taxi outside the Desert Inn and slammed the door. "Take me to the Desert Inn," he commanded.

The disgusted driver got out and opened the back door. "You're in front of the Desert Inn now, buddy," he snapped.

Devlin looked at the nitery and turned to the hackie. "Okay," he muttered, "but next time don't drive so fast!"

*　*　*

It was Ryan's 104th birthday. Reporters gathered around him and one of them asked the routine question, "To what do you attribute your long life?"

"I have never touched a drop of intoxicating liquor!" answered the old Irishman.

Suddenly, from the next room, there came a tremendous crash, followed by a barrage of angry shouts.

"Good heavens, what was that?" cried the reporter.

"Oh," explained Ryan, "that's my father. He always makes a lot of noise when he's drunk!"

"Why is tea more popular in England than it is in Ireland?"

"Have you ever tried Irish Coffee?"

\* \* \*

O'Yeery was really loaded. His doctor said to him, "Don't you know drinking shortens a man's life?"

"Yes," he hic'd, "but he sees twice as much in the same length of time."

\* \* \*

Hennilly was brought into night court, not just for being drunk but also on suspicion that he was the notorious night prowler. "What were you doing out at three A.M.?" asked the judge.

"I was going to a lecture."

"A lecture at three o'clock in the morning?" asked the judge.

"Oh, sure," said Hennilly. "Shometimesh my wife shtaysh up longer than that."

Cuddihy was blotto and stumbling along Boyle Street at 4:30 A.M. panic-stricken. A cop stopped him and said, "Do you have an explanation?"

"If I had an explanation," slobbered Cuddihy, "I'd be home with me wife!"

* * *

McHatton and Kildare were weaving their way home one night.

"Shay," said McHatton, "won't your wife hit the ceiling when you walk in tonight!"

"She probably will," said Kildare, "She'sh a loushy shot."

* * *

Shea and McCormick were sitting on a curb in the wee small hours of the night.

"Watsch your wife shay when you shtay out thish late?" asked Shea.

"Haven't got a wife," said McCormick.

"Then watsch the idea of shtayin' out sho late?"

In Manhattan, a policeman strolling his early morning beat stopped in front of an East 80s brownstone. Sitting on the stoop was Milarney, completely snookered.

"Why don't you go on home?" suggested the cop.

"I live here!" said Milarney.

"Why don't you go inside then?"

"I lost my key," answered the drunk.

"Why don't you ring the bell?"

"I did . . . an hour ago!"

"Why don't you ring it again?" asked the officer.

"The hell with 'em," snorted Milarney, "Let 'em wait!"

*"Let 'em wait!"*

O'Flynn stumbled into the house around four in the morning. He was only half drunk, partly dressed, smeared with lipstick and smelling of cheap perfume. "Hello, darlin'," said O'Flynn to his wife.

"How dare you," screamed Mrs. O'Flynn, "come into the house in that condition, when we're goin' to a funeral tomorrow?"

"A funeral," said O'Flynn. "Whose?"

"Yours," she replied.

\* \* \*

Did you hear about the Irish drunk who picked up a hairbrush, looked at it, and said, "Guess I need a shave."

\* \* \*

"You want to know why I've come home loaded?" sputtered O'Malley.

"Yes," said his wife.

"Because I ran out of money, that's why."

McNellis shuffled home one night in a drunken stupor, carrying the biggest ham Mrs. McNellis had ever seen.

"Now, then, out with it," she exclaimed. "Where'd you get that ham?"

"Won it at the tavern, drinkin' with the boys, me darlin'."

"And how did you come to win it, may I ask?" she continued.

"Me love," said McNellis proudly. "It was given to the man with the biggest organ. Everyone at the bar opened up and . . ."

"Kevin Patrick Michael McNellis!" shrieked his wife. "You don't mean to tell me you took out that whole thing in front of everybody?"

"Now, darlin'," said the Irishman, "not the whole thing. Just enough to win."

\* \* \*

"I have a money problem which is causing me drink problems," said Mulroy.

"Why is that?" asked Culkeen.

"I never have enough money to buy all I want to drink."

Bryant, the bartender, loved boxing. Two customers got him talking about John L. Sullivan and his great fights. Meantime, they kept ordering drinks and each time Bryant tried to collect, one of the men said, "Eh, you rang it up!"

After the two cheaters left, O'Neill, who'd been watching their trick, tried the same thing. "Now hold on," said the bartender, "don't be givin' me any of that boxing routine!"

"What boxing? What routine?" asked O'Neill. "Just give me my change and let me out of here!"

\* \* \*

Flattery got really potted at the neighborhood barroom and had to urinate. Unfortunately, he couldn't remember whether he had buttons or a zipper on his fly, so he asked McAndrew to help him to the toilet.

McAndrew pretended to unzip him, but shoved a banana into his hand from the free-lunch counter and pushed him into the cubicle.

Flattery peed, lifted his hand, looked

wildly at the banana, and felt the wetness down his legs. He lurched back into the bar screaming, "My God! I tore my pecker out at the roots and I'm bleeding to death!"

* * *

Rizzutti was sitting in the neighborhood bar. Next to him sat McIntyre who had had more than enough beer and was staring at his empty glass. He turned to Rizzutti and asked, "Shay, did jou shpill a glash of beer on me?"

"Absolutely, no!" answered the Italian.

McIntyre turned to the man on his other side. "Mishter, did jou any chance throw a glash of beer in my lap?"

"No!" snapped the man.

"Jusht what I been sushpectin'," said the Irishman. "It'sh an inside job!"

* * *

"What were his last words?"

"He said, 'I can't figure out how they can make anything on this stuff at three dollars a pint.'"

# OVERHEAD AT SKELLY'S SALOON

*"We don't have TV but we do have fights every night."*

\*　　\*　　\*

McGonigle climbed off his stool at the bar and dragged himself into the men's room. Suddenly he began howling and the bartender came racing in.

"Every time I flush this thing," stammered the Irishman, "it bites me!"

"Of course it does," said the bartender. "You're sitting on the mop bucket."

\*　　\*　　\*

*Henehan* (to stranger in saloon toilet):
Shay, is my peter out?
*Stranger:* No, it isn't.
*Henehan:* Well, it ought to be. I'm pishin' as fasht as I can.

A huge bully sauntered into the dimly lit saloon. "Is there anybody here called Kilroy?" he snarled. Nobody answered. Again he sneered, "Is there anybody here called Kilroy?"

There was a moment of silence and then a little Irishman stepped forward. "I'm Kilroy," he said.

The tough guy picked him up and threw him across the bar. Then he punched him in the jaw, kicked him, slapped him around and walked out. About 15 minutes later the little fellow came to. "Boy, did I fool him," he said. "I ain't Kilroy."

\* \* \*

Delaney, the New York saloon keeper, found his cash was always short. One day he said to his bartender, "George, did you take any money out of the cash drawer last night?"

"Yes, I took my carfare home," he replied.

"An' whin did ye move out to Los Angeles?" asked the Irishman.

Ferguson and Malone decided to go hunting one morning. "Listen," said Ferguson, "I'll bring all the guns and such, and you bring all the provisions."

"Fine," said Malone.

The next morning when they met, Ferguson was loaded down with guns and ammunition. Malone was carrying a loaf of bread and six bottles of whiskey.

Ferguson blew his stack. "Look what happens when I leave the provisions to you!" he shouted. "A loaf of bread and six bottles of whiskey! What the hell are we gonna do with all that bread?"

*"What're we gonna do with
all that bread?"*

The customer put $5 on the bar counter and staggered away. Hallahan put it in his pocket and turned to find the boss glaring at him.

"Would you believe it," said Hallahan, "he leaves a $5 tip and doesn't pay for his drink."

* * *

Dr. Mead, a lecturer on the evils of drink, put two glasses in front of him—one filled with water, the other with whiskey. He then dropped a big worm into the water. It swam about in contentment. Then Dr. Mead took out the worm and put it into the whiskey. In a few moments the worm wriggled and died.

"That," said the doctor, "is what happens to your insides when you drink whiskey!"

The audience was quite impressed, especially old Mrs. Kilgallon. After the lecture she waddled up to Dr. Mead and said, "What brand of whiskey did you use?"

"Why do you ask?" said the doctor.

"Because," she said, "I've been bothered with worms for years."

28

# THE $64,000 QUESTION

*Why is it Irish drunks never spill drinks on other Irish drunks?*

\* \* \*

"I'm against liquor. That was the cause of my father's death."

"Drank too much?"

"No. A case fell on his head."

\* \* \*

Dr. Willis tried to convince Millarney that he should give up drinking.

"Ever notice a cactus plant?" he asked the Irishman. "If you pour water around its roots it thrives, turns greener and grows bigger. Take the same cactus plant. Pour vile liquor on it and what happens? It shrivels, it shrinks, it dies. Doesn't that teach you anything?"

"Yes," said Millarney. "If you want a cactus growing in your stomach, drink water."

## MACUSHLAH MAXIM

*An Irishman isn't drunk as long as he can hold on to a blade of grass without falling off the face of the earth.*

Gilluly and Kehoe were getting ready to go on a hiking trip.

"I'm taking along a gallon of whiskey in case of rattlesnake bites," said Gilluly. "What are you taking?"

"Two rattlesnakes," answered Kehoe.

*　　*　　*

*Social Worker*: The last time I came here you made me very happy because you were sober.

*McClanahan*: Thash true, honey. But today, it's my turn to be happy.

*　　*　　*

A motorcycle cop stopped a speeding truck that had been weaving down the highway and asked the driver his name. "It's on the side of the truck," the driver told him.

The policeman said, "It's obliterated."

"The hell it is," replied the driver. "It's O'Brien."

Shanahan staggered out of the saloon. He wandered up the street and by mistake went into a house where a wake was being held. He spotted the refreshments and helped himself.

The wake lasted all through the night and well into the next day. Shanahan made himself useful by serving as bartender and always had one with the guy who was drinking.

At the end of the second day the party thinned out quite a bit, until at last Shanahan was alone with the widow. She approached him for the first time.

"You must have been a great friend of O'Leary to stay on like this," she said sadly, "so I feel I can ask your advice. Do you think we should take poor O'Leary to a funeral home or should we hold the services here?"

Shanahan took a final swig of gin and said, "Missus, why don't we just stuff him and keep the party going?"

\* \* \*

Mrs. Vandercook, the temperance lecturer, pounded the lectern as she warned

the audience about the evils of booze.

"Who is the richest man in town?" she shouted. "Who has the biggest house? The saloon keeper! And who pays for it all? You do, my friends, you do!"

A few days later, Houlihan, who had been in the audience, met Mrs. Vandercook on the street and congratulated her on the effectiveness of her speech.

"I'm glad to see that you've given up drinking," said the woman.

"Well, not exactly," said Houlihan. "I just bought a saloon."

\* \* \*

Inebriated old Kincaid, swaying unsteadily and his arms flailing wildly, flagged down a bus on the corner.

"Driver," he cried when the door was opened for him, "do you go to Forty-shecon' Shtreet?"

"Yes, I do," said the driver.

"An' Broadway?"

"That's right, Forty-second and Broadway."

"Well, g'bye," waved the juiced-up Irishman, "and have a good time!"

A fire engine streaked down the street, its siren shrieking, when Madigan came stumbling out of a saloon.

He chased the fire truck for three blocks shouting, "Stop! Stop!" Finally, out of breath, he dropped to the pavement and shook his fist.

"All right for you," hollered Madigan, "you can keep your lousy old peanuts!"

*　　*　　*

Margaret got smashed at the company's Christmas office party. The sales manager, Harvey, offered to drive her home. She staggered out to his car, gave him her address and away they drove.

Fifteen minutes later, she leaned over and said, "Harv, you're passionate." Immediately he reached for her thigh. Margaret slapped his face.

They drove in silence, and then . . . "Harv, you're passionate," and again he reached for her thigh. Pow! He stopped the car and said, "Look, honey, on one hand you tell me I'm sexy, on the other you whack me across the mouth. Make up your mind!"

Margaret looked at him and slobbered, "Who the hell said you were sexy? All I've been telling you is, my house, you're pashin' it."

Herb Beatty, Pittsburgh's peerless interior decorator, cracks up clients with this cajoler:

Pittman was taking his grandfather clock to be repaired and carrying it under his arm. Turning a corner, he walked head-on into bleary-eyed Bannon and they both went sprawling to the sidewalk.

"Why the hell don't you look where you're going?" shouted Pittman.

"Oh, yeah," said Bannon. "Why don't you carry a wristwatch like everybody else?"

*Why'ncha carry a wristwatch
like everybody else!"*

# THE ETHNIC TRUTH

*When drinking, a Frenchman wants to dance, an Englishman wants to eat, an American wants to talk, and an Irishman wants to keep drinking.*

\* \* \*

Shanley's legs were paralyzed and the doctor was putting him through a lot of tests.

"Look, Doc," said Shanley, "set a glass of whiskey on that table over there. If I don't make it, I'm helpless."

\* \* \*

Ahearn ambled into the house to the amazement of his wife. "What happened?" she asked. "You've never come home drunk before. How'd you get this way?"

"Two Scotsmen ruined me," declared Ahearn.

"Who were they?"

"Haig and Haig!"

# GILLHOOLEY'S GOSPEL

*The horse and mule live thirty years*
*And know nothing of wines or beers.*
*The goats and sheep at twenty die*
*With never a taste of scotch or rye.*
*The cow drinks water by the ton*
*And at eighteen is mostly done.*
*The dog at sixteen cashes in*
*Without the aid of rum or gin.*
*The cat in milk and water soaks*
*And then in twelve short years it croaks.*
*The sober, modest, bone-dry hen*
*Lays eggs for nogs, then dies at ten.*
*The animals are strictly dry;*
*They sinless live and swiftly die,*
*While sinful, ginful, Irishmen*
*Survive for three score years and ten.*
*And some of us, though mighty few,*
*Stay pickled till we're ninety-two.*

\* \* \*

*Coyle:* Boy, did we throw a big party in
our cellar last night!

*Dyer:* You don't say! Was your cousin
Aloysius there?

*Coyle:* Was he! He was the big party we
threw in the cellar.

O'Callahan, the motorcycle cop, helped direct traffic for a large wedding reception. Later the bride's father invited him in for some liquid refreshment. Officer O'Callahan put away almost a quart of bourbon and went back to his duty in a slightly inebriated state.

O'Callahan proceeded to hang overtime parking tickets on 74 cars before he found out he had wandered into a drive-in movie.

*     *     *

O'Houlihan traveled up and down a train, putting his head in every compartment and asking for a priest. He appeared quite upset and when he came back for a second time, a Methodist minister said: "We are all brothers in the Lord. Although I am a Methodist minister, if you will take me to your friend who is ill or distressed, I will comfort him as well as I may."

"It's meself that's after bein' distressed!" said the Irishman.

"What can I do for you, brother?"

"Nothing! I gotta have a priest. I need a bottle opener."

# THROWIN' THE BULLS

*A "bull" is a complete confusion of concepts, an incongruity of ideas. Webster calls it "a grotesque blunder in language." Bulls have been attributed to the Irish, possibly because of Obadiah Bull, an Irish attorney, who practiced in London during the reign of Henry VII.*

*Lawyer Bull was supposed to have been a notorious blunderer. These "bulls," passed on and nourished by time, have become an integral part of the Irish comic spirit. The following are some classic examples:*

The happiest man on earth is the one who has never been born.

\* \* \*

It's a good thing for your wife that you're not married.

41

No Irishman will ever allow himself to be buried in any but an Irish cemetery. He'd rather die first.

\* \* \*

Health is a wonderful thing to have, especially when you're sick.

\* \* \*

He remarked in all seriousness that it was hereditary in his family to have no children.

\* \* \*

They were crossing a bridge.
"Hello, Casey, how are you?"
"Not too bad, Mullarkey. But my name isn't Casey."
"Well, mine isn't Mullarkey, so it mustn't be either of us."

"There are people dying this year who never died before," reported an Irish coroner.

\* \* \*

"Dear Molly," wrote Cassidy, "this is the fourth letter I've written to you asking for your hand in marriage. If you still refuse, please return this letter unopened."

\* \* \*

The orator wound up his speech: "You may have children; or, if not, your daughters may have."

\* \* \*

"You're such a pest," said Garrigan to his misbehaving child. "The next time I take you out I'll leave you home."

## SIGN OUTSIDE DONEGAL
## DANCE HALL

LADIES AND GENTLEMEN ARE WELCOME,
REGARDLESS OF SEX

\* \* \*

Then there was the Irishman who was asked the difference between an explosion and a collision.

"In a collision," he replied, "there you are, but in an explosion where are you?"

\* \* \*

The archbishop had preached a rousing sermon on the beauties of married life. Two buxom Irish ladies left the church feeling uplifted and contented.

" 'Tis a fine sermon His Reverence gave us this morning," observed one.

"That it was," agreed the other, "and I wish I knew as little about the matter as he does."

"Isn't it a pity that the MacGuires have no children, Mr. Flynn?"

"It is indeed, but I hear that sterility is hereditary in both sides of their family."

\* \* \*

O'Shay was standing at the curb when McGinty, a friend from his old home town whom he hadn't seen in years, approached. They embraced, but McGinty seemed mighty serious. "I'm awfully sorry to tell you this," he said, "but your dear old Aunt Edith is in jail."

"Glad you told me," said O'Shay. "It's good to hear she's provided for."

\* \* \*

An Englishman, a complete stranger to Dublin, was on a bus and asked Haggarty, the passenger beside him, if he was right for the Town Hall.

"Quite correct," said the Irishman. "This bus goes to the Town Hall. You get off at the stop before I do."

Cullen and Horgan went hunting. A big bird flew up in front of them and perched on a tree staring down at them. Cullen aimed his gun and Horan shouted out, "Don't shoot yet, Cullen! The gun ain't loaded!"

"Can't help it, Horgan, the bird won't wait!"

*"Can't help it, the bird won't wait!"*

*"When I tell you how beautiful this colleen is, you won't believe it! And I don't blame you 'cause it's a lie!"*

\* \* \*

Pat: The trouble with my cousin Danny is he has no backbone.

Mike: I don't agree with you. He's got backbone enough if he'd just bring it to the front.

\* \* \*

Passing a cemetery one day, Reagan paused at a tombstone. He read the words, I STILL LIVE.

"Bejabbers, if I was dead I'd be honest enough to own up to it!"

The theatre was crowded and the Irish attendant, unable to find a seat for the pretty young girl, said to her:

"Indade, Miss, I should like to give you a seat, but the empty ones is all full."

*　*　*

"I'm neutral," said Doolan in a Dublin pub one day during World War II.

"Yes? And for whom are you neutral?" challenged the other man.

*　*　*

"An' poor O'Sull got 16 years in jail."

"What for?"

"For hommycide, I belave."

"Oh, that's nothing; I thought it might be for killin' somebody."

"Poor McMilligan, Faith, I'm afraid he's goin' to die," said Grogan.

"And why would he die?" asked his friend.

"Oh, he's got so thin! You're thin enough, and I'm thin—but, by my soul, McMilligan is thinner than both of us put together."

\* \* \*

"Gentlemen, isn't one man as good as another?"

"Sure, he is, and a great deal better!"

Moynihan was brought to court by his better half on a charge of wife-beating. Mrs. Moynihan told the judge, "Every night when this bum comes home he takes this baseball bat here and hits me over the head a couple of times, just to warm up. Then he goes after me with his fists for awhile, and when he gets tired of that, he uses a rolling pin to beat me with. Judge, this bum is a bum, that's all."

"You've heard your wife's evidence," said the judge. "Now what have you to say in your own defense?"

"Your Honor," said the Irishman, "Don't pay no attention to this woman. She's punch-drunk."

\* \* \*

"Mrs. Lafferty," said the doctor, "you've had ten children. Enough is enough. As a birth control method I want you to sleep with your feet in a two-gallon pot."

Two months later she became pregnant again. "Well, doctor," she explained. "I didn't have a two-gallon pot, so I used two one-gallon ones."

"Now Mrs. Donahue," asked the attorney. "You say your husband has never said a kind word to you since you were married? Are you sure of that?"

"Come to think of it," she replied, "once in a while he did say 'You're a foine one.' "

\* \* \*

"Did you hear that I'm engaged to an Irish lad?"

"Oh, really!"

"No, O'Reilly."

\* \* \*

"If I married you, Molly, would your father give you the dowry?"

"Yes, Sean."

"And do you think he'd let us live here if we got married?"

"Yes, Sean."

"Would he let me be the manager of the hotel as well, if we married, Molly?"

"Yes, Sean."

"Will you marry me, Molly?"

"No, Sean."

Marcia Smith-Durk, the delightful *Dallas Times Herald* reporter, donated this dash of drollery:

Kate and Terence, from a small town in Ireland, decided to honeymoon in Dublin. They rented a bicycle-built-for-two and went sight-seeing.

After riding around for 20 minutes, Terence said, "I don't understand this thing, it's awfully hard to pedal."

"What I don't like," shouted Kate from behind him, "is the way these foot rests keep moving up and down."

\* \* \*

John Robins, the brilliant British television and motion picture director, gets guffaws from cast members with this jolly jest:

In Donegal, Kathleen was arrested for disturbing the peace. At the police station she indignantly refuted the allegation until the sergeant pointed at her open blouse.

One breast was completely exposed.

"Oh, Mother of God," she cried, covering herself, "I've gone and left me baby on the bus."

The McQuinlans, an innocent honeymoon couple right from the heart of Connemara, were shown to their hotel room. It had twin beds.

"Oh, Mac," cried the bride, "why can't we have a room to ourselves?"

* * *

Mrs. McQuinlan, the newlywed, looked at the list of mealtimes in their hotel:

*Breakfast*—6:30 to 11:30

*Lunch*—12:30 to 3:30

*Dinner*—6:30 to 9:30

"Mac," wailed the bride, "sure we'll be kept in eatin' so long we won't have time to go anywhere."

* * *

"Is it true you've been courtin' the widow, Campbell?"

"Yes, I've been kissin' the back of her neck, but I won't any more!"

"Why not?"

"My teeth keep gettin' caught in her wrinkles!"

Gilfoyle was sitting in a station smoking, when Mrs. Nugent came in and sat next to him.

"Sir, if you were a gentleman," she said, "you would not smoke here!"

"Lady," he said, "if ye wuz a lady ye'd sit farther away."

"If you were my husband, I'd give you poison!"

"Well, Lady," replied Gilfoyle, "if ye wuz me wife, I'd take it."

\* \* \*

*There was an old widower, Doyle,*
*Who wrapped up his wife in tinfoil.*
*He thought it would please her*
*To stay in the freezer—*
*And, anyway, outside she'd spoil.*

\* \* \*

## SOUTH BOSTON IRISHMAN'S
## LOVE SONG

*Ireland must be heaven, because my wife isn't there.*

Malcolm Shore, the dynamic service director for Dixon Cadillac in Hollywood, dug up this doozy:

The widow Bourke had been picking the weeds around her husband's grave, when she was tickled in the crotch by a stalk of wild oats. "Oh, me poor darlin'," she sighed, "you're still as horny as ever!"

*"Still horny as ever."*

Haggerty's wife woke in the middle of the night to hear him moving things about in the kitchen.

"What might ye be lookin' for?" she asked.

"Nothin'," said Haggerty. "Just nothin'."

"Oh!" said his wife. "Then ye'll find it in the bottle where the whiskey used to be."

\* \* \*

*Hart* (to his wife) : You're drunk, woman. You can't even hold your liquor!

*Wife* (clutching bottle) : Oh yeah! Let me see you take it away from me!

\* \* \*

A temperance worker rang the Cudahy doorbell.

"Good morning," he said. "I'm collecting for the Inebriates' Home and . . ."

"Why, me husband's out," replied Mrs. Cudahy, "but if ye can find him anywhere's ye're welcome to him."

McDonnell came upon his good friend Brannigan in the cemetery and heard him mumble over an old, unmarked grave, "Why did ya' have to die? Why did ya' have to die?"

McDonnell felt bad for his friend, so he went up to him and said, "Who is it you be mournin' after all these years? Yer mother, or yer father?"

"No," Brannigan replied tearfully, " 'tis me wife's first husband."

\* \* \*

Kevin Hagen, the talented television and motion picture actor, tells about Flanagan's funeral. The priest, who had never met the Irishman, delivered an overly long complimentary eulogy over the coffin. As he kept heaping compliment on compliment, the widow Flanagan became restless and embarrassed.

Finally she nudged her son, sitting next to her and said, "Go up and look in the coffin and see if that's your father in there."

"I'm afraid, Mrs. O'Day, your husband will never work again," said the doctor sadly.

"I'll go in and tell him. It might cheer him up."

* * *

Keen-witted Roger Kennedy, the Independent News Company's super salesman for the Colorado territory, came up with this cackler:

Gallagher and his family were walking to the cemetery with the body of his recently departed wife. Suddenly, one of the pallbearers tripped on a cobblestone and fell. The casket dropped to the ground and opened.

Everyone stood in shock as the dead Mrs. Gallagher opened her eyes. She was very much alive, the victim of catatonia.

Five years went by and Mrs. Gallagher passed away, this time a victim of natural causes. But Gallagher had not forgotten, and on the way to the cemetery as the pallbearers approached the spot where her casket was dropped, he shouted, "For God's sake, watch the cobblestones!"

# WEARIN' OF THE GREEN

Kerrigan was painting a house and working very fast. A neighbor asked him why he was in such a rush.

"I'm trying to get through," replied the Irishman, "before the paint gives out."

* * *

Shannon applied for a job as a keeper at the San Diego Zoo. On the application form he came to the question, "What is rabies and what can you do about it?"

Shannon's answer: "Rabies is Jewish priests, and you can't do anything about it."

"Mrs. O'Skelly," said the landlord, "I've decided to raise your rent."

"Ah, now," beamed Mrs. O'Skelly. "It's the darlin' ye certainly are. I was wonderin' how I could raise it meself."

*　*　*

The boss sent for his new secretary, Miss Brady. "Listen," he said angrily, "you gotta always answer the phone the minute you hear it ringing!"

"If you say so," said Miss Brady. "But it all seems so silly. Nine times out of ten it's for you!"

*　*　*

## ST. PATRICK'S DAY

*A wonderful occasion that gives the Irishmen the same feeling of omnipotence Texans have all year round.*

*　*　*

Milbank, a first-time visitor to Boston, stopped Anderson, a black man sitting in the common. "Excuse me," said Milbank, "do you know the quickest way to get to City Hospital?"

"Yes, suh," replied the black man. "Just walk up to the nearest crowd of white folks and say, "To hell with the Pope!"

\* \* \*

## SHAMROCK CALENDAR

*First comes St. Patrick's Day when the Irish celebrate the Wearing of the Green.*

*Then comes April 15th—when the government observes the Sharing of the Green.*

\* \* \*

The foreman looked at the applicant for work.

"Are you a mechanic?" he asked.

"No, sorr," was the reply, "Oi'm a McCarthy."

\* \* \*

*There was an old girl from Kilkenny*
*Whose usual charge was a penny.*
*For half of that sum*
*You could roger her bum,*
*A source of amusement to many.*

"What kind of a detective is McQuade?"
"Well, one time a burglar robbed a safe wearing calfskin gloves. McQuade took the fingerprints and five days later he arrested a cow in Chicago."

*"...five days later he arrested
a cow in Chicago!"*

Shaughnessy worked in a poor mining town in West Virginia. He and his wife had never traveled anywhere. One day Shaughnessy won a fortune in the Irish Sweepstakes and decided that he and the Mrs. would sail to Ireland to celebrate their windfall.

Aboard ship their story soon became known and on the second day out, the steward said to them:

"The captain would like you to join him at his table tonight."

Shaughnessy said to his wife, "How do you like that? Here we are payin' $3000 for this voyage and they want us to eat with the crew!"

\* \* \*

"What's become of yer pretty niece Mamie?"

"Oh sure an' the girl's married a lord."

"Why, an English lord?"

"Faith, an' what would a good Irish girl be doin' with an English lord? 'Tis an American lord she married—a landlord who keeps a motel in Hoboken."

*There was a young woman named Riley*
*Who valued old candle ends highly;*
*When no one was looking*
*She used them for cooking.*
*"It's wicked to waste," she said dryly.*

\* \* \*

Burke: At what age wuz yer mother married?

Nolan: At fourteen.

Foley: I can beat that. My mother wuz married at thirteen.

Evans: Faith, I can beat y'all. My mother wuz married before I was born.

\* \* \*

Phelps was telling his cousin of a narrow escape during the war. "The bullet went in me chest and came out me back," explained Phelps.

"But," said his relative, "it'd go through your heart and kill you!"

"Oh, no!" said Phelps. "Me heart was in me mouth!"

*Brian:* The very first time I saw you, something went through my head!

*Colin:* Why not! There's nothing *to* stop it.

\* \* \*

McCarran opened his first bank account and began paying for everything by check. One day his statement came from the bank. The Irishman didn't understand it but the returned checks pleased him.

"Sure, an it's a smart bank I'm doin' business with!"

"Why's that?" asked Mrs. McCarran.

"Oi pay me bills wid checks an' be jabbers if the bank wasn't slick enough to get every check back for me."

\* \* \*

"This America is a great country."

"And how's that?"

"Sure'n, the bank sez you can buy a twenty-foive dollar money order for 50¢."

*The cheer of St. Patrick's Day comes at the right time—just before April 15th when tax payments leave us all a little green around the gills.*

\* \* \*

Mr. Finkelstein entered his Shaker Heights home and said to Agatha, the new maid, "Can you tell me of my wife's whereabouts?"

"Sure an' I believe they're in the wash," answered the young Irish girl.

\* \* \*

Over the years there have been many enormously funny fluffs made by radio and TV announcers. One of the most quoted was made by a CBS newscaster when he introduced New York City's Irish mayor as, "His Honor, Meyer O'Dwyer!"

Bailey the beggar came over, holding out his hand, "Please give a poor old blind man 50¢."

"But you can see out of one eye."

"Then make it a quarter."

\* \* \*

*There is a young girl of Kilkenny,*
*Who is worried by lovers so many*
*That the saucy young elf*
*Means to raffle herself,*
*And the tickets are two for a penny.*

\* \* \*

There are those that believe the Irish have a stubborn nature and this story might back up that claim.

Sweeney met Bracken on the road. "Where you off to?" he asked.

"I'm goin' to Connemara," replied Bracken.

"You mean you're goin' to Connemara, God willing."

"No, I'm goin' to Connemara, God willing or not."

Because of this presumptuous remark Bracken was turned into a frog and kept in a pond for several days. When he had completed his penance, Bracken was changed back to his original form. Returning home, he began packing his belongings again.

"Where're you goin' now?" asked Sweeney.

"I'm goin' to Connemara."

"You mean you're goin' to Connemara, God willing."

"No!" shouted Bracken. "I'm goin' to Connemara or back to the frog pond."

*　*　*

Because of his rare blood type, Gaffney was selected to be the donor for an English king who had been seriously ill.

The first transfusion helped enormously. A second brought the stricken ex-monarch back to consciousness.

The third was in progress when the king jumped up in bed and shouted, "The hell with the King of England!"

Francis Dlugowski, Pittsburgh's celebrated Marine Corps War hero, sent in this silly spirit lifter:

McBride got a job at an observatory. During his first night's duty he paused to watch a learned professor who was peering through a large telescope. Just then a star fell.

"Man alive!" exclaimed the Irishman. "You're a foine shot."

*"You're a fine shot!"*

*Brian*: There's only one difference between you and a jackass. A jackass wears a collar.

*Colin*: But what do you mean? I wear a collar!

*Brian*: Then there's no difference.

\* \* \*

"Alma!" shouted Reardon to his secretary.

"Yes, sir."

"Take a letter to my lawyers, O'Brien, O'Brien, and O'Brien. Dear Mr. Ginsberg . . ."

\* \* \*

"How is your son the doctor doing in Dublin, Mrs. Dunleavy?" asked the curious neighbor.

"To tell you the livin' truth, he's makin' so much money that he doesn't have to operate on every patient now."

McManus, the new gardener, gazed wonderingly at the shallow basin containing water on the lawn.

"What's that for?" he asked Nora the maid.

"That's a bird bath!" she explained.

"Now don't be foolin' me!" said McManus. "What is it really?"

"A bird bath," repeated Nora. "Don't you believe me?"

"No!" declared the Irishman. "I don't believe there's a bird alive that can tell Saturday from any other night!"

\* \* \*

Carmen Fields, the terrific top lady in Los Angeles's Try Foundation, tells about the American tourist visiting Dublin. He stopped Finnerty, the mailman. "Do you think it is going to rain?" asked the tourist.

"When God was running our country," replied Finnerty, "I could always predict the weather right. Now with the government running it, nobody can predict anything!"

Daniels was walking along a Dublin street when he was addressed by aged Mrs. Fennelly who was selling thread. "Help a poor old lady and buy some thread," she pleaded.

"I don't sew," said Daniels.

"And neither shall ye reap," said the old woman.

\* \* \*

Brian: Isn't this an awful picture of me? I look just like a monkey!

Colin: You should've thought of that before you had it taken.

\* \* \*

Lanahan, a new policeman in Belfast, found a dead horse in Chichester Street.

"How do you spell Chichester?" he asked some of the people around him; but nobody in the crowd knew.

"All right, then," said the cop, "somebody give me a hand to pull the animal onto Oak Street."

Old Rafferty married a colleen 30 years his junior and soon afterward died of a heart attack, leaving the poor girl penniless.

Rafferty's friends and neighbors decided to hold a raffle to raise money for the young widow.

McCarran, the chairman, met Calhoun coming out of the saloon. "We're havin' a big raffle for the widow Rafferty," said McCarran. "How about you buying a ticket?"

"I'd sure like to, but I couldn't," said Calhoun. "My wife wouldn't let me keep her even if I won her!"

\* \* \*

An Englishman traveling in Kilkenny arrived at a ford and hired a boat to take him across.

In crossing he asked McDermot the boatman if anyone had ever been lost in the passage.

"Never," replied McDermot. "My brother was drowned here last week, but we found him the next day."

Hartley, the foreman of a gang of railway men, found one of his men asleep. With a smile, he said, "Sleep on, ye idle bum, sleep on. So long as ye sleep ye've got a job, but when ye wake up ye're out of work."

* * *

*Fogarty*: Did you go over ta visit Kelly in the hospital last night?

*Costigan*: No. After I'd walked tree quarters of the way, I decided it was too far to go, so I turned around and went home.

* * *

As Gilligan and McCullen were walking through the cemetery they stopped to look at a tombstone upon which was inscribed: NOT DEAD, BUT SLEEPING HERE.

"He's decieving no one but himself," said Gilligan.

"Glory be, here's a long liver for you,"

said McCullen as he looked at another stone. "It says here 175; what an age!"

"Yes," said Gilligan as he also stopped to look. "Name's Miles from Dublin."

\* \* \*

"Three cheers for Home Rule!" roared Kavanagh after a rousing political rally.

"Three cheers for Hell!" cried a Scotsman.

"That's right," replied the Irishman, "every man should stick up for his own country."

\* \* \*

"Bridget, stop on your way home and see if the butcher has pigs feet."

Bridget returned an hour later, without a package. "Didn't he have them?" asked the mother.

"Faith, mum, his trousers were so long I couldn't see whether he had pigs feet or not."

McClosky arrived in the U.S., having left his wife in Dublin after he promised her that he would send for her once he was settled and had found a job.

Six months later, he received a letter from his wife. McClosky couldn't read so he asked his foreman at the construction site to read the letter.

In a loud, gruff, gravely voice, the foreman bellowed aloud the contents of the letter:

"WHY HAVEN'T YOU SENT FOR ME? I NEED MONEY! HAZEL."

McClosky angrily grabbed the note and stuck it in his pocket. The following Sunday at church, the immigrant was chatting with his priest, Father Dillon.

"Have you heard from your wife?" asked the clergyman.

"Sure, Father," replied McClosky. "Here's a letter she sent to me."

The priest read the note out loud in a soft, gentle voice, "Why haven't you sent for me? I need money. Hazel."

"Are you going to send for her soon?" asked Father Dillon.

"I wasn't last week," replied the Irish immigrant. "But now that she's changed her tone, I'll send her the money tomorrow."

"Pat, why did you enlist in the 34th Regiment?"

"To be near me brother who's in the 33rd."

*   *   *

Immigrants McKern and Garrett arrived in New York. On their first night they were pestered with mosquitoes and they couldn't sleep. Finally, about 2:00 in the morning, when they were both weary from their efforts to keep the pests off, a firefly happened to sail through the open window.

"It's no use," said McKern. "Here comes one o' the critters searchin' fer us with a lantern!"

*   *   *

*A disgusting young lad named McGill*
*Made his neighbors exceedingly ill*
*When they learned of his habits*
*Involving white rabbits*
*And a bird with a flexible bill.*

Frank O'Connor, the lovable Hollywood General Studios exec, lights up the lot with this lulu:

Officer O'Shea was doing his best to stop scraper.

a man from jumping off a New York sky-

"Think of your sweetheart," O'Shea shouted to the fellow.

"I haven't got one," he replied.

"Think of your father and mother," pleaded the cop.

"I'm an orphan," shouted the suicide.

"Think of the saints of Ireland," begged the Irishman.

"Why should I? I'm English."

"Go ahead and jump, you bastard!"

*"Jump, you bastard, jump!"*

What do they call a fag in Ireland?
Home O'Sexual.

* * *

Armstrong developed severe stomach cramps and, unable to reach the public toilet, had to relieve his bowels in the park. Armstrong noticed Officers Tooley and Branahan approaching, so he quickly covered the pile with his hat.

"Good morning," said Armstrong. "Could you help me?"

"Of course," said Patrolman Tooley.

"I'm a visiting ornithologist, and I've caught a rare bird under this hat. Could you guard it while I get a cage from the zoo?"

"You can trust us," answered Officer Branahan.

After several hours of standing guard, with no cage arriving, the policemen decided that one would lift the corner of the hat very carefully, and the other would make a wild grab at the bird. Tooley lifted the hat and cried, "Have ye got him?"

"Faith an' begorra," replied Branahan. "I've busted every bone in his little body!"

Holligan's mother-in-law complained of a miserable toothache. "The best remedy for toothache," advised Holligan, "is to fill your mouth with cold water."

"Yes, and then?"

"Then you sit on the stove. When the water boils, your toothache will be cured."

* * *

Mrs. Muldoon, expecting her 12th child, decided that the time had come to tell her children about the blessed event. Assembling them that night in the living room, she broke the news.

"The stork," she said happily, "will be coming to pay us a visit!"

"A visit!" said Mr. Muldoon, looking up from his newspaper. "What do you mean visit? He lives here."

* * *

Brian: When was the Declaration of Independence signed?
Colin: I never was too good in geography.

Handsome John Conte, the genial Palm Springs host of KMIR's Talk Town, gets tall titters with this tail-wagger:

Father Mulcahey had just checked into the hotel. The bellboy had taken up his suitcase, then showed him how to turn on the television set and operate the thermostat. He indicated the bathroom with a grand sweep of his hand, turned over the key, and delicately kept his hand outstretched.

Father Mulcahey shook it.

The bellboy coughed and said, "It is customary, Father, to give a small gratuity on an occasion like this."

"My son," said the priest, "I'm afraid I have no money, but tell me, are you a drinking man now?"

"Yes, indeed, Father."

"In that case, my boy, kneel down and as a gratuity, I will have you take the temperance pledge."

*"Kneel down, boy, and I will have you take the temperance pledge!"*

Duffy and McDowell were riding in the country when their car broke down. They stopped at a nearby store. "How far is it back to New York?" asked Duffy.

"Twenty miles," replied the clerk.

"We'd better get goin'," said Duffy. "Twenty miles is a long way to walk."

"That's not so much," said McDowell. It's only ten miles apiece!"

\* \* \*

Private Lenihan, his head swathed in bandages, was being given his morning coffee rectally. Suddenly he began to grunt and wave his arms.

"What's the matter?" asked the nurse. "Too hot?"

Speaking out of the side of his mouth, Private Lenihan said, "Too much sugar!"

\* \* \*

A company of Irish soldiers was sent by the UN to keep peace in Africa, and Ser-

geant Kleenan was briefing them.

"Now, men," he said, "if you are bitten by a snake, the first thing you must do is cut the place where you've been bitten so that it bleeds freely; then apply your mouth to the cut and suck out as much blood as you can."

"But, Sergeant," interrupted Private O'Connor, "suppose you are bitten on the backside."

"In that case, me bucko," said the NCO, "it'll be then you'll know who your friends are."

*  *  *

"Well, my boy," asked Ryan's father, "how do you like being married?"

"Married? Ha, some marriage," answered his newlywed son. "I married a nun."

"What do you mean, a nun?" asked his father.

"None in the morning, none at night," replied the groom.

"Well," sighed Papa, "come for dinner Friday night, you'll meet the Mother Superior."

# THE SAINTS BE PRAISED

In the confessional, Cavanaugh confessed that he had kissed MacNamara's wife.

"So you committed this sin, did you?" said the priest. "Did you kiss Mrs. MacNamara more than once?"

"Father," said Cavanaugh. "I'm here to confess, not brag!"

\* \* \*

Father McCord was writing the certificate at a christening, trying to remember the date. He said to the mother, "Let me see, this is the nineteenth, isn't it?"

"The nineteenth, bejabers! Yer Reverence must be losing your mind. This is only the eleventh I've had."

Young Maureen knelt in the confessional and whispered to the priest:

"Oh, Father, I've sinned grievously. On Monday night I slept with Shamus. Tuesday night I slept with Timothy. On Wednesday night I slept with Dennis. Oh, Father, what shall I do?"

"My child," replied the priest, "go home and squeeze the juice from a whole lemon and drink it."

"Oh, Father, will this purge me of my sin?" she asked.

"No, child, but it will take the smile off your face."

\* \* \*

Just after World War II, all the nuns but one in a French nunnery were found to be pregnant. The bishop did some investigating and learned that the nuns had all been raped by German soldiers.

Nevertheless, he interviewed the one skinny nun who was not pregnant. "But why didn't they rape you?" asked the priest.

"Well," she said, "I resisted."

When the Vatican heard that a Dubliner was the father of 25 children, a special medal was struck for him and was delivered by a local priest.

" 'Tis very nice of the Pope," said the proud father, "especially as I am not a Catholic."

"What!" shouted the enraged priest, "do you mean to tell me that His Holiness has had a special medal struck for a sex-crazy Protestant!"

\* \* \*

After 10 years of wedded bliss, Hennessy and his wife had 9 children. The priest talked to the Irishman about the difficulty of raising such a large family, and suggested he practice restraint.

Then babies number 10 and 11 came along. The padre collared Hennessy again and asked, "Have you been using *restraint?*"

"That I have, Father, for the last two years," replied Hennessy, "but what's a man to do, when he wakes up in the middle of the night, and the missus is helping herself?"

Father Kernan stopped Gannaway on his way into the church.

"Could you come back tomorrow night for confession? We have hundreds in the church right now. You haven't committed a murder since the last time?"

"Indeed I haven't, Father," said Gannaway. "I'll come back tomorrow night."

On his way out he met McClain.

"Go home, McClain, and come back tomorrow. They're only hearing the murderers tonight."

\* \* \*

Sally Quick, IND's super midwest rep, came up with this colorful quip:

Father McKee, minister to an impoverished district, was the beneficiary of a gift day, in which all parishioners brought gifts up to the altar.

The priest rose to thank them. "An' one thing that touched me heart most of all," he said, "was when little Maggie Clancy walked up the aisle and laid an egg on the altar."

One Sunday, Coogan sat in his pew oblivious to the remarks being made from the pulpit. What Coogan failed to hear, among other things, was the announcement that there would be three collections on this particular morning—one for the church, one for the school, and the third, a special collection for the missions.

When the basket came by the first time, Coogan dropped in a dime. The second time, it came around he came up with another dime.

Coogan was startled out of a deep daydream by the third presentation of the collection plate. "What the devil are they gonna do next," he cried, "search us?"

\* \* \*

"That was a beautiful hat your wife wore to church this morning," remarked Gannon. "It was so high I could hardly see the pulpit above it."

"It should'a been beautiful," replied Gannon. "An' if she'd worn the bill that come with it, you wouldn't a seen the steeple!"

*There was a young monk from Siberia*
*Whose morals were very inferior.*
   *He did to a nun*
   *What he shouldn't have done*
*And now she's a Mother Superior.*

\* \* \*

A priest who had two churches to serve decided to hold baptismal services at both parishes. He told his secretary to place an ad in the paper, announcing the fact. It appeared like this:

"Rev. Father Dugan will hold baptisms at East End Church Tuesday morning; at West End Church Thursday; and the following Wednesday at 11 A.M. and 3 P.M., children will be baptized at both Ends."

\* \* \*

Father Murray saw a small boy standing on tiptoe trying to reach a doorbell. The priest climbed up the stairs and rang the bell for the lad.

"Thanks, Father," said the youngster. "Now let's run like hell!"

Garrigan was working on the construction of a new building. The foreman said to him one day, "Didn't you tell me once that your brother is a bishop?"

"Yes, sir," replied Garrigan.

"And you a hod carrier! The good things of this life are not equally divided are they?"

"No, sir," said the Irishman. "Poor fellow! My brother couldn't do this to save his life!"

\* \* \*

Lucille Wilson, the lovely Los Angeles Security Pacific Bank exec, like this lopsided laffer:

Kelsey was being interviewed by St. Peter at the Gates of Paradise.

"Sure it's a snap ye have here, Saint Peter," said Kelsey, "holding down this soft job century after century."

"Ah, but you must bear in mind," said St. Peter, "that in Paradise a million years are but a moment, and a million dollars are but a cent."

"Thin will ye be loaning me a cent?"

"Certainly, in a minute!"

Tommy Moore, the talented Philadelphia comic and recording star, tears audiences apart with this titillator:

During a Sunday service at the church, one pretty member of the choir seated in the balcony became so wrought up with the spirit of the occasion that she leaned out too far and fell over the rail. Her dress caught on a nail and she hung suspended in mid-air, revealing all.

The thoughful priest cried out, "Any man who dares look will be stricken blind!"

McGonigle turned to his friend and said, "I'm goin' to chance one eye."

*"I'm goin' ta risk one eye!"*

In a small town they had just erected a fine new church. All it needed was a set of chimes. So Father McLain went around collecting donations for the chimes. Deegan, the blacksmith, donated $50; Dugan, the contractor, came across with $75; Donnelly, the undertaker, gave his check for $100. When the priest got to Brennan's Bar and Grill, the owner didn't like the idea of contributing $200.

"But Brennan," said the priest, "just think—Deegan, Dugan, and Donnelly gladly contributed to the chimes. And you should be represented with a donation."

"Well, Father, it's an awful lot of money."

"But think how proud you'll feel, along with Deegan, Dugan, and Donnelly, when the chimes ring out."

The saloon keeper finally agreed and when the chimes were installed, the Reverend met Brennan on the street. He said, "Brennan, did you hear the chimes?"

"I heard them."

"What's the matter, don't you like them?"

"Well, I hear them ring out Deegan, Dugan, Donnelly; Deegan, Dugan, Donnelly . . . but doggone it I never hear anything that sounds like Brennan!!!"

Kyle Milligan, San Jose's sophisticated storyteller, gets screams with this silly:

A just-ordained priest was feeling fairly cocky. He was riding along in his car at 70 miles an hour when a motorcycle cop pulled him over and the cop started writing out a ticket. "But, officer," said the priest, "I'm Father Fox!"

The cop said, "I don't care if you're Mother Goose! I'm giving you a ticket!"

\* \* \*

*Parson*: I intend to pray for you to forgive Bragan for having thrown that brick at you.

*O'Grady*: Maybe you'd be saving yer time, Reverend, if you'd just wait till I get well and then pray for Bragan.

\* \* \*

*A young Irish pansy named Perch*
*Had developed a taste for the church*
*    And monks, priests, and preachers,*
*    And such horny creatures*
*Were the constant MEANS of his search.*

Mrs. Tumulty walked up to Cartwright, the clerk in a bookstore, and asked him to recommend a book she might like. He grabbed the nearest book, entitled, "The Kentucky Cardinal."

"I don't read Catholic books," said Mrs. Tumulty indignantly.

"But, Madam," said Cartwright, "this cardinal is a bird."

"I don't care what he is," said the Irish woman, "I still don't read Catholic books!"

\* \* \*